MISOGYNY IN PSYCHOANALYSIS

MISOGYNY
IN PSYCHOANALYSIS

Michaela Chamberlain

PHOENIX
PUBLISHING HOUSE
firing the mind

First published in 2022 by
Phoenix Publishing House Ltd
62 Bucknell Road
Bicester
Oxfordshire OX26 2DS

British Library Cataloguing in Publication Data

A C.I.P. for this book is available from the British Library

ISBN-13: 978-1-912691-39-5

Typeset by Medlar Publishing Solutions Pvt Ltd, India

www.firingthemind.com

For Augusta, Beattie, and Beckett

Contents

Preface

When I started my training in psychotherapy, I was introduced to some of the writing of the key thinkers in psychoanalysis and I was instantly fascinated by the world that seemed to be opening up before me. I became an avid reader, and vividly remember my first experiences of reading highly recommended papers and books. Often the patients the authors described (more often than not, '*his*' interactions with '*her*') seemed out of this world—literally. In my previous twenty years' experience of working in mental health, I had never met anyone as these analysts described them, in fact I had never met anyone, anywhere, as certain authors depicted them.

The more I read, learnt, studied, and have sat with many people in therapy sessions during my training and subsequently working as a psychotherapist, I have come to realise that there was something in my initial instinct about the other-worldliness of these well-regarded analysts' patients. The 'otherness' was not to do with the extraordinary magic of psychoanalysis, though at times psychoanalysis can be magical. It was more due to the symptom created by the inherent misogyny in psychoanalysis—a desire for there to be a world that one can be on the outside of, an exclusive club where the main 'otherness' is, and always has been, aimed at women.

In psychoanalysis misogyny hides in plain sight, seemingly above and beyond the usual conventions of workplace etiquette or even a vague awareness of sexism. It is commonplace in psychoanalytic literature and in the presentation of case studies for a description of the, usually female, analysand's attractiveness to be given as a diagnosis rather than an opinion, for the word 'feminine' to be used as a synonym for submission, for psychosexual development to miss the glaringly obvious important stage of menstruation, for a child's development to be modelled on the Freudian theory of male psychosexual development, for women to still be described in terms of their loss of not having a penis but gaining a baby—not a vagina or clitoris, and for the fundamental experiences of pregnancy, birth, and menopause to continue to be overlooked. Ironically for a field whose main currency is reflection, the different treatment of women is bypassed because misogyny is institutionalised in psychoanalysis. As has happened to many psychoanalysts since the time of Freud, a refusal of this misogyny means that you then step outside of the purely psychoanalytic field and are then relegated to a 'niche' group usually described as 'feminist', thereby becoming no longer a threat to the tradition of psychoanalysis. This has happened many times over and it is with no irony that in writing this short book I am fully aware that my contribution may also be relegated to a subdivision that moves it far away from psychoanalysis and ensures it is buried under a very heavy carpet. I hope not.

Psychoanalysis is an extraordinary discipline in which, at its heart, there is a desire to make a genuine connection with, and have a full understanding of, another person's experience, but it is at its worst when it is hierarchical and 'othering', sharing in jokes—because in order for something to be 'in' the price to be paid is having to leave something or someone 'out'. Misogyny in psychoanalysis is too important to leave anything or anyone out of the conversation, precisely because it is about everyone, not *just* women.

This book is short because I would like it to be the start of a conversation that should be accessible for anyone who has an interest in psychoanalysis or in the impact of misogyny when it is allowed to spread unhindered. I use the terms psychoanalysis, psychotherapy, analyst, and therapist interchangeably as whilst acknowledging the difference between these terms, I would also not like to further the hierarchy that is often implicit in these terms especially as many therapists work in a way that would be considered analytical and vice versa. I have also used the terms woman and man, male and female to include anyone who identifies with these terms and would like to be clear that whilst I have included menstruation, pregnancy, and childbirth as being part of the experience of being a 'girl' and 'woman' this is intended in both its presence and its absence in both the physical and the psychical sense, and therefore applies to all people who identify with this gender.

The book reflects my experience in the world of psychoanalysis and psychotherapy as a trainee, supervisee, student, teacher, psychotherapist, and supervisor in various institutions and as a former Chief Executive of a psychotherapy organisation. My wish in writing this book is to extend an invitation for you to join me in putting psychoanalysis on the couch and to be curious about why it is the way it is. Psychoanalysis is remarkably resistant to applying its own treatment to itself and is well defended. In writing these pieces the feeling was often with me that I was doing something wrong, speaking out of place, and sticking my head above the parapet until I discovered how much this was a symptom of the psychoanalytic misogyny I had internalised. More importantly, I realised that that needed to change, not just for myself, but for a discipline that could offer so much more if it decided to change too.

CHAPTER ONE

The mansplaining of psychoanalysis

#medbikini was trending on Twitter in the summer of 2020 with women medics posting pictures of themselves in bikinis. The hashtag was in response to a study published in an American medical journal which was conducted by a mainly male team, which described doctors who shared photos of themselves on social media in 'inappropriate attire' such as pictures in underwear, provocative Halloween costumes, and posing in bikinis/swimwear as 'unprofessional'.

The report reignited a familiar debate of what constitutes 'appropriate attire' but the response that it mobilised undercut the seemingly innocent guideline around what is suitable to wear in the workplace, which has usually centred much more around what it is suitable for women to wear in the workplace as against what men should wear. The finding that it was 'unprofessional' for medics to be seen in bikinis could be more simply interpreted as a control on being a 'woman' in the workplace— her physical presence and difference from men is tolerated as long as she is not 'too' physically (and therefore mentally and emotionally) female.

The controls around what can be worn of course usually apply to all members of the workforce, but the difference is in the practicality of the guidance, men traditionally being expected to wear trousers and flat shoes, and women expected to wear skirts and sometimes shoes that are uncomfortable and physically damaging (in 2017, the UK Government rejected calls to outlaw company bosses forcing female employees to wear high heels).[1] The control over workwear allows a not-so-micro aggression against women, drawing attention to what she is wearing, instantly undermining who she might be or what she might have to offer to her profession beyond dress sense.

In the world of psychoanalysis, it is exactly these unconscious processes that one might expect to be addressed and where there is great opportunity, and always has been since Freud first described the unconscious, for understanding the roles men and women play, and have been ascribed, in society. It has been an ongoing discomfort for me that I never really felt like I was properly confronted by sexism and, as argued by Manne,[2] its lawgiving arm, misogyny, until I trained as a psychotherapist.

I have undertaken psychoanalytic training in various institutions and had the opportunity to be supervised by well-established supervisors in the field who identify themselves as male or female. Prior to training as a psychotherapist, I had worked in mental health and learning disabilities for over twenty years, so when I say that I wasn't properly confronted by misogyny until training as a psychotherapist, I mean that I had never had the direct experience in a professional context of being treated as a 'single story' or reduced to a stereotypical image of my chosen gender, which is female.

When I read the story of certain clothing being described as 'unprofessional' it reminded me of an experience retold to me by a trainee whilst in the very early stages of training as a psychotherapist. She had been offered an interview for a psychotherapist position with a highly regarded clinic; she considered herself fortunate to have been invited. Excitedly she told her supervisor the news and was keen for his insight as to what the interview might entail. After congratulating her, he immediately asked what she was going to wear. Confused by the question (as she was used to dressing for professional environments) and feeling slightly awkward, she asked why and commented that it had not been at the forefront of her mind; her supervisor then proceeded to suggest different 'outfits' she could wear and imagined out loud what her interviewer, also a woman, might be wearing. When she enquired as to what he thought she might be asked at the interview, he bluntly replied that she would want to know if she were 'sane', no further suggestions added. In a scene that seems more fitted for the 1970s, where a man in his fifties gives fashion advice to a woman at least ten years younger than himself, it was a surprise for me that this took place just over five years ago.

I could have taken many things from that story, such as an expectation that no matter how I develop in the profession of psychoanalysis, senior, prominent male analysts will still not have taken the time to analyse their own misogyny and when threatened will reduce me to an 'outfit' too. I was instead more intrigued by how such a conversation was seen as acceptable and the feelings it evoked in me. However, I still remember the shock and the not-so-gentle feeling of being pushed down as the story was told to me and how the trainee had been made to feel 'less than'. The shock is the same as the one that still jolts me when I hear psychotherapists who are also teaching on training courses caution against women who wear lip balm as they are unconsciously 'softening the spite-filled words they are about to speak' or to be aware of women wearing red nail varnish as they are 'murderous women'. This is not to deny that these interpretations have the potential to resonate with unconscious material in some people but perhaps the real caution should be around the loss of subjectivity which should signal that the psychotherapeutic process has collapsed.

The story of psychoanalysis began with men trying to understand women through the study of hysteria and more significantly through the lens of male experience, with male experience being seen as the 'norm'.[3] Freud developed his theories based on case studies from other clinicians, his self-analysis, and through the analysis of his patients, the vast majority of whom were women. In the hundred years since the inception of psychoanalysis many of Freud's theories have been challenged, redescribed, abandoned, and indeed defended in bitter battles. The place of women has been amongst these battles, has been at times prominent, at times less so. But with a striking consistency, there is a remarkable disappearing act that takes place for the women who have taken part in these battles and more importantly their contributions have been dismissed or relegated to a 'special interest', a parallel process for what has happened generally to women in psychoanalysis. What is more of note is that in the one arena where unconscious processes should be thought about, the givens of patriarchy challenged, the roles of women and men understood within the cultural context of sexism and misogyny, the world of women has become just that—the 'world' of women, a split-off group separated from the patriarchal 'norm' of men. The fact that writers who challenge the role of women in psychoanalysis either self-label as feminist, or are labelled as feminists, reflects that the mainstream remains non-representative of women's experiences; the mainstream implicitly is that of Freud's classical psychoanalysis but tweaked and evolved.

The question in this is if the mainstream is 'Freudian 2.0', then does that also mean that we are accepting a mainstream psychoanalysis that is inherently misogynistic, where the male experience dominates and is still taken to be the 'norm'? Furthermore, if that is the case then why is psychoanalysis protecting a blind spot of misogyny?

From Freud's description of women as 'the dark continent',[4] psychoanalysis has continued to try to grapple with the place of women. In 1950 the British psychoanalyst Winnicott wrote about the 'fear of women',[5] conceptualising this fear as one of dependency and indebtedness to what was given to you by your mother in the early stages of life; Bowlby in describing what is needed for a secure base[6] to exist has been heavily criticised for placing the mother as being needed in the home;[7] and notably women analysts have argued with the traditional phallocentric model of psychosexual development from Karen Horney in the 1920s contesting Freud's view of penis envy,[8] to ongoing developments in feminist perspectives in psychoanalytic theory. But there seems to be a gap in relating the theory to clinical practice. Whilst dealing with the unconscious processes which are conceptualised and attended to with the prejudice of the analyst's own theoretical framework and the impact of their own analysis, something has been lost of women's lived experience. I am curious about how much of the blatantly concrete is missed in the privileging of the unconscious and therefore how much this blindspot consequently impacts on the unconscious. The fundamental fact of women working in a patriarchal society, being trained within that system without a proper analysis of what that means and the impact that has on us as women, is overlooked. (It has still never been fully explained to me why Melanie Klein is often referred to as 'Mrs Klein', but yet Freud and Winnicott are never given their title of 'Mr'.)

To gain an insight into the current context of women, as Freud advises, the best way of understanding psychoanalysis is to look at where it has come from and how it has developed.[9] The historical context is not to further join the many criticisms of Freud's phallocentric view of psychosexual development but more to show the long shadow thrown by these theories on the women in his time and in the generations that followed him. What seems crucial to this is the time frame: it has been over a hundred years since the formalisation of a psychoanalytic movement. However, the time quickly condenses when one considers that those who formed this movement were then the analysts and supervisors of the next generation who furthered the theory, any dissent regarding the theory of female psychosexual development being quickly quashed.

Within the traditional world of British psychoanalysis much importance is often placed on the analyst's psychoanalytic heritage, for instance, by whom they were analysed during their training and in turn by whom their analyst was analysed, often hitting the jackpot if the lineage can be traced back to one of the main analysts such as Klein, Winnicott, Anna Freud, or Sigmund Freud himself. Given that Anna Freud died in 1982, Winnicott in 1971, Klein in 1960, it is possible to have only one or two 'degrees of separation' from these icons within the field. The importance of this is the identification with these people and of course with their thinking and writing, the identification giving the analyst a sense of authority and security in their own thinking. It is this identification which I think is also crucial in the justification and continuation of misogyny within psychoanalysis.

As I later discuss in Chapter Three, 'Freud bingo', Freud's original theory of psychosexual development was based on an assumption of women lacking and wanting what a man possessed.[10,11] According to Freud, denial of this by either sex would have serious consequences for their development. In a way, Freud set up the perfect double bind for anyone wanting to disagree, as their disagreement would be a sign of not having achieved this basic developmental milestone. Women would have to accept their place, or this would be pathologised and it took Freud and the many other analysts who followed him to 'explain' this to women. If women wanted to be fully part of the psychoanalytic movement then they would need to adhere to this thinking, or perhaps better described, the female analysts would need to swallow this misogynistic trauma.

It is this trauma that has been carried by women and passed on between the generations, of numbing out the injury caused, and averting one's psychoanalytic gaze from the obvious downgrading of women so as to not lose the connection with Freud. The American psychoanalytic sociologist Professor Nancy Chodorow[12] gave an example of this 'numbing out' when she interviewed some of the early women psychoanalysts. She met with Margaret Mahler who trained as a psychoanalyst in the 1920s, knew members of Freud's close circle, and went on to become a renowned analyst and theorist. When Mahler was asked by Chodorow about her experience and how Freud's theories corresponded to her own life, a blind spot emerged; the place of women was so far out of the main view that it did not even occur to Mahler to apply Freud's theories to her own life, she commented 'it didn't go through my brain'. It is this internalisation of the misogyny that paralyses thinking, as explored later in 'The misogynistic introject', that continues to pass on the trauma through the generations.

Freud's theories and subsequent variations on his views of women have by no means gone unchallenged, but what is without doubt is the absence of women and their experiences to have a proper seat at the psychoanalytic table, instead being given a seat at the occasional table brought out for special events. A simple literature review shows an absence of psychoanalytic writing on the fundamentals of a woman's lived experience such as menstruation, pregnancy, and childbirth.[13] This is not to reduce women's experience to these three facts or to define the female gender by physical processes, but more as an illustration that even the obvious, stereotypical, female processes that were of course in existence in Freud's time, have been far from the forefront in psychoanalytic thinking.

It has been suggested that this absence is due to a lack of interest, which could be the case, but the real question that I wanted to explore through writing these essays, particularly in Chapter Two, 'Still face', and Chapter Five, 'The missing period in psychoanalysis', is why there is a lack of 'interest' especially in a field where Freud's daughter gained prominence and the main divergence from Freudian thinking came from another woman, Melanie Klein. As Chodorow points out, throughout the 1920s to 1970s in the UK, this field was populated with a high proportion of female therapists and analysts and yet it was driven by men.[14] Today, even a cursory glance at directories to find analysts and therapists or a visit to a psychoanalysis conference will show that men are in the minority. There is something incongruous in the lack of challenge against the place of women in psychoanalysis. Moreover, even when that challenge is made, it is not incorporated into the mainstream.

A common dismissal and sometimes defence of Freud is that he was a 'man of his time'. This is often used as criticism by those who are repelled by his ideas or offended by the way in which he describes women and female development, but perhaps more concerning, it is often used as an explanation for why he conceptualised women in such a way. The explanation implies a sense of it being acceptable that he would view women as 'lesser', that this would be so entrenched and not even worthy of consideration; yet the explanation is being applied to someone who is considered to be one of the greatest thinkers of the twentieth century, who radically placed sexuality in childhood and was clearly committed to listening to the women he saw rather than dismissing them as 'mad' and seeing the unconscious processes that had sought to resolve the women's distress.

There have been different ideas about why Freud came to the view that women were lacking in comparison to men, ranging from his defence against anti-Semitism, his relationship with his youngest daughter Anna,[15] to his immersion in the culture and medical training of his time.[16] What is clear is that whatever Freud's motives and processes for presenting a theory of the Oedipus complex,[17] he maintained his thinking about this area of child development even in the face of opposition from women analysts, who presumably had more personal insight than Freud on female development. The frustration for the female analysts must have been tremendous as their own feelings and emotions were effectively 'mansplained' to them by Freud and his almost exclusively male entourage. The Oedipus complex took centre stage for Freud and was almost a 'no go' area for disagreement; he saw it as fundamental to psychoanalysis and anyone who disagreed was edged out politely or not so politely from his group.[18]

The inherent misogyny of the Oedipus complex was not a grey area, nor was the demand for those who wanted to be followers of Freud to comply. As anyone who has read Freud will testify, this insistence in adherence to this theory and a lack of change is especially of note; one of Freud's great skills, and a great challenge in reading him, is following the many changes he makes to his ideas as he reviews and updates his theories as his thinking develops. However, what is also of note is that despite sticking to theoretical descriptions of female development and applying these theories in his work with patients, he also continued to write of his lack of understanding of girls and women, famously writing in 1926:

> we know less about the sexual life of little girls than of boys. But we need not feel ashamed of this distinction; after all, the sexual life of adult women is a 'dark continent' for psychology. (p. 212)[19]

Karen Horney was one of the first analysts to openly disagree with Freud about his version of development with the girl envying the father's penis. In 1924, writing about Freud's theory of female development, her objection was clear:

> (it) amount(s) to an assertion that one half of the human race is discontented with the sex assigned to it … it is decidedly unsatisfying, not only to feminine narcissism but also to biological science. (p. 51)[20]

Horney found support in Ernest Jones who also disagreed with Freud, but it was Horney, whose growing frustration with Freud's theory of penis envy and lack of response from him, who pushed the disagreement and eventually was punished for her dissent. In 1941 she was dismissed from the Psychoanalytic Institute in New York for teaching 'heretical ideas'; those deciding her fate at the Institute were men who were closely linked to Freud.[21] Horney then disappeared from the psychoanalytic literature; even in Ernest Jones's autobiography, with whom she had been heavily involved in the dispute with Freud, she is barely mentioned.[22]

Horney was not the only woman to disagree with Freud. The first female member to be accepted to the Vienna Psychoanalytic Society, Margarete Hilferding also voiced her dissent. In her first and only presentation to the group in 1911, she spoke of the mother not just as being the caregiver for the baby but also as a woman and sexual being. Hilferding also did the unthinkable and spoke of the physical impact of childbirth, something that from a contemporary perspective would be expected to be of interest to psychoanalysis, given the rich material childbirth provides when thinking of the unconscious impact this may have on the mother. However, this was dismissed out of hand by Freud as 'the only way to find out something about mother love can be only through statistical examination'.[23]

The way these two women were treated in the early stages of psychoanalysis seems to have set the tone for further understanding of women. Both women were treated in the entitled manner of men who presume to know more than women about their own experience and with the presumption that women are the aberration rather than the norm. Freud, throughout his writing, alludes to something that is not known about women, something that is beyond his reach and he is well aware of his lack of understanding.[24] However, his seeming resignation to this, due to the difficulty of understanding women, seems to have translated for some in the psychoanalytic community into the understanding of women was not so important, and for some the understanding of women has become locked in a time capsule with Freud's thinking. A startling example of this is in a paper by Denis Hirsch in the 2018 book *Psychic Bisexuality*, edited by the current president of the British Psychoanalytical Society, where he refers to his female patient's[25] penis envy:

> the "female hollow" is the site of female castration ... This hollow also evokes the function of receptivity and passive—active dynamics that characterize the female organizing fantasy. (p. 187)[26]

This example illustrates that whilst many analysts since Horney have continued to contest Freud's views and to reimagine the psychosexual development of women within a less male-dominated framework, many of the arguments have taken place within their own socially distanced bubble, the impact of the writing bouncing off other bubbles and seen as not belonging to them.

Part of Freud's legacy in psychoanalysis is the establishment of a system whereby it is acceptable for men to presume to know better than women about their experience whilst simultaneously acknowledging that they themselves do not know that much. I recently attended a public seminar where a male psychoanalyst presented a case history of an impasse between himself and his patient. He talked about the woman falling in love with him, the challenges of holding this within the therapeutic relationship, and the meaning of the relationship for both him as the analyst and her as the patient. The analyst considered that this impasse was worked through when the woman accepted that he would always have more love for psychoanalysis. This was presented as a good working through of a very involved piece of work. What was perhaps missed, I would suggest because it was presumed a given, was that the 'good' working through was a restoration of a temporarily disrupted patriarchal order, the man's love for a theoretical, intellectual construct being more important than love for a woman sat in front of him. She had become too active and moved out of a submissive role, taking charge of the relationship; the resolution was achieved when she returned to being submissive and realising her place within the hierarchy. My interpretation of events of course could be mistaken, or not what was experienced by the female patient and male analyst, but what I find more interesting is that in the course of a two-hour presentation and discussion, this was not even considered. The female patient's feelings were reduced to simply 'being in love' with the analyst, no further exploration required.

There has been a continued effort to present a female perspective on women in psychoanalysis, however it is not within the scope of this book to provide a detailed analysis of the many varied and significant contributions of many psychoanalysts (predominantly female) who have taken forward the thinking about women in psychoanalysis. There is a long history starting with Karen Horney who battled directly with Freud, Clara Thompson in 1940s, the impact of first-, second-, and third-wave feminists with writers who have transcended the different generations of feminist thinking such as Muriel Dimen, Jessica Benjamin, Nancy Chodorow, Joan Raphael-Leff, Joyce McDougall, Rosemary Balsam, Susie Orbach, and Luise Eichenbaum.[27] There have been works such as Orbach's *Fat is a Feminist Issue*[28] which have put women, their bodies, and the perception of women centre stage, as well as developments such as the journal *Studies in Gender and Sexuality*, founded by Goldner and Dimen in 2000 with the specific intention of not holding with the usual Freudian tenets around women.

Significantly, as pointed out by the British doctor, psychoanalyst and Yale Professor of Psychiatry Rosemary Balsam, in a paper whose title describes perhaps how many women have felt about how they have been treated, 'The war on women in psychoanalytic theory building: past to present',[29] there is a:

> manic-depressive rhythm of response (that) echoes the classic rhythms of interest in female issues in the upsurge of focus, excitement, and enthusiasm that is followed by a more enduring level of symptomatic ennui on the topic in our field. (p. 102)

It is as though thinking about women comes in and out of fashion without the obvious question being asked of why this is happening in psychoanalysis and what are the unconscious or conscious processes at work that are allowing this to happen. I question why there is not more anger and outrage about this.

It is of note that in 2018 Rosemary Balsam was the first US woman to receive the prestigious Mary Sigourney award honouring outstanding Psychoanalytic Achievement Worldwide, almost thirty years after the award was eponymously founded by a woman in 1989.[30] Of the awards that have been presented to date, ninety-one of the recipients have been men; twenty-two women have been given the award, almost a quarter of the number of male recipients. The number of women awarded is only fractionally ahead of the nineteen organisations that have received the Sigourney Award.[31]

In organisations where women are in the majority it would seem that there is a discussion to be had about the internalised misogyny that is enabling and allowing the dominance of one gender over another. This in turn, of course, needs to feed into the much larger debate about gender in general and how we treat and define each other on the basis of difference or similarity, not just in case studies and theoretical constructs, but in the way this permeates through psychotherapeutic establishments.

CHAPTER TWO

Still face

In 1974, Marina Abramović performed *Rhythm 0*,[1] a piece in which she stood still for six hours and, most importantly, remained expressionless. In the room where she stood was a table on which seventy-two individual items were carefully displayed including amongst other things a feather, pieces of food, perfume, a knife, gun, and bullet. Over the table were the instructions:

'There are seventy-two objects on the table that one can use on me as desired.'

'I am the object. During this period I take full responsibility.'

At the start of the piece, the audience entered the room and were bemused by Abramović, making playful attempts to get a response from her, but as time progressed and without a reaction from her, the playfulness turned into aggression. The audience pushed the boundaries between themselves and the motionless artist, trying to get beyond her expressionless façade, literally getting into her by piercing her skin with pins, pushing thorns into her head; one man cut her skin and sucked the blood coming from the wound. As the unresponsiveness continued, the aggression and desire to get inside her, to get something more than an expressionless face, intensified. She was stripped, laid out on a table, and a knife was stabbed into the wood between her legs.

Abramović was left physically scarred by this experience and the then twenty-six-year-old artist was left emotionally marked feeling that the main learning from the performance was that 'the public can kill you. If you give them total freedom, they will become frenzied enough to kill you'.[2] At the end of the six-hour piece, she 'came to life' and started walking towards the audience at which point they all ran away from her, perhaps in fear of retribution from her, or perhaps more wanting to run away from their own difficulties of reconciling their anger with a withholding woman and that the same woman may also have feelings of her own about how others make use of her.

Rhythm 0 is sometimes taken as a damning statement about human nature: if one takes away responsibility then the 'dark side' of being human is unleashed, as though the real meaning of being human is Freud's 'death drive',[3] without a governing superego, all that is left of human desire is aggression and destruction with an overarching need to sever connection. From this standpoint, once the façade of civility is removed then we all return to a narcissistic state, following our own desires without any regard for anyone else. This view may make sense if it is following the Freudian idea that we are all born into a state of primary narcissism,[4] but it unravels when the presence of the mother is included. The infant's physicality is intimately shared with the mother from the moment of inception; the infant is dependent on a relationship with the mother from before birth, being born into a state of relatedness more than one of narcissism.

However, Abramović's experience in *Rhythm 0* is perhaps better understood away from Freudian destructiveness and placed more suitably in the context of the origins of human relating. In the same year as her performance, similar research into human responsiveness and relating was taking place in the form of the 'still face experiment'. Instead of adults experiencing the expressionless, unresponsive face of Abramović, the clinical psychologist and psychoanalyst Ed Tronick,[5] asked mothers to present an expressionless or 'still' face to their babies and observed what happened. What they observed in one mother and baby was seen in many other mothers and babies. The baby responded, in the same way as Abramović's audience, initially greeting the lack of response from the mother with playfulness, trying to charm a reaction out of the mother in front of him. When this failed, the baby tried harder to get a response by giving more exaggerated hand gestures, making louder noises but as the time progressed the baby became increasingly distressed, the baby's limbs started to flail around, turning his head sharply away from the still face and trying to move out of his seat in a combination of fear and despair until eventually collapsing into tears.[6] All of this takes just a few minutes as against the six hours of Abramović's performance.

The raw uninhibited response of the baby gives a strong indication of the internal importance of the maternal gaze. In the absence of language, the gaze and responsiveness of the mother is essential in communicating to the baby that the mother is fully present; the baby is present in the mother's mind and gives the baby a sense of cohesion, containment, and most importantly of being able to find herself in the mother's face. The British psychoanalyst Winnicott, in 1952, wrote that 'there is no such thing as a baby',[7] meaning that the baby does not exist on its own, it is always in, as he described it, 'a unit'[8] with the mother. However, what this underestimates is the significance of the mother's and the baby's separate subjectivities and crucially that an aspect of the mother as a grown woman will always be separate and not enmeshed with the baby.

Winnicott's mother and baby unit is heavily unbalanced, the baby dependent on the mother not just for her physical needs to live but also for her psyche to survive through her attachment to the mother. The baby being able to find herself in the mother's facial expression is essential for a sense of existence and survival. However, the mother is not dependent on the baby for her survival; she may be dependent on the baby for her well-being, but the dependency is not the same. As described by Bion, in the same period as Winnicott, the mother carries out the essential work of taking in the infant's raw feelings and states of being and makes sense of them in a way that can be understood by the infant.[9] The mother may need to do this for her own sense of self as a mother but of course, if her childhood was good enough, she would have already experienced this being done for her and gone on in later life to find other people with whom she can experience this in a more adult form, finding herself in relation to their reactions.

Crucial in this is that the infant is not able to do this for the mother; the infant needs the mother for a sense of existence, not the other way round. Tronick et al.'s research found the baby's response was important for the mother in that there is an aspect of mutual emotional regulation. This finding is clear for most observers of mothers and babies, who experience almost infectious contentment in seeing a mother and baby play together when there is enough space in their relationship for both of them to be present in the interaction. It is this mutuality of being open to receive each other that is key in the connection being created between the two. All things being equal, the mother, of course, already has the skills to initiate this kind of interaction and uses these skills when also interacting with other people. The baby, however, is learning them from the mother and is dependent on her to translate both the baby's and her own experience into a language they both understand. At this stage of development, the baby's full expression and sense of self is mediated by the mother.

Abramović's performance reignited this early existential dilemma of needing to find oneself in the primary carer, the feelings of dependency, the need for a response, and more importantly the pain of not receiving it. The removal of responsibility from the audience and placing herself as the female central 'object' with ultimate authority—it is she who decided that the audience would have no responsibility—replayed this primary relationship of mother and infant. Her lack of response became unbearable, dysregulating the entire audience. Abramović described how, at one point, the 'madness' of the audience overtook the room as the security guards intervened to remove a loaded gun that an audience member had placed in her hand, pointing it at her own head.[10] In that moment the security guards, no longer able to contain their own feelings, suddenly intervened and grabbed the gun, throwing it out of the window. In an act that seemed to want to stop the anger and aggression towards Abramović, it feels closer to say that the act was one of a wish for the audience to throw away their aggression; the lack of response from this mother figure was intolerable.

From a certain perspective it could be argued that *Rhythm 0* as a concept is deeply boring: a woman stands in a room for six hours with a table with objects on it. Nothing is promised. The object of interest is not actually what the artist does, it is more in what she fails to do; the real performance is the lack of affect and the torturous feeling this elicits in the observer which in turn results in real peril for both the performer and the observer. The real performance is in the genuinely unbearable need for a response and the sense of dislocation for the self when the self cannot be found in the other.

This peril, and creation of it, is something that is familiar to all psychoanalysts since Freud recommended placing the patient on the couch and sitting behind them where the patient was unable to see the analyst's face. Freud's reasons for this were intriguing, in that there was something that he too found unsettling about his—predominantly female—patients' gaze. The famous reason he gave for encouraging the use of the couch was that he found it too uncomfortable to be stared at all day, later explaining that this also helped the patient to speak freely, without being influenced by the facial expressions of the analyst. Freud was also aware of the difficulty that this lack of responsiveness caused, advising on how to manage patients who may protest about having to lie on the couch. The anxiety that this power imbalance created was intentional for Freud as it is still in current use. For some analysts, the patient being unable to bear this anxiety causes some people to be diagnosed as 'unanalysable', unsuitable for psychoanalysis. This diagnosis not only misses something crucial about analysis, in that it is not just about being 'anxiety resilient', but also misses something fundamental about being human—the need to be physically as well as emotionally seen.

As demonstrated by Abramović and Tronick, the need for a responsive face is intrinsic to safety, relating, and, to state the obvious, a sense of existing—the opposite of not being acknowledged is accurately described in common usage as 'being ghosted', pointing to the feeling of being dead/non-existent if one is not recognised by the other. The prototype for this recognition by the other has been, traditionally, for the vast majority of people, the gaze and attention of the mother as primary carer. As shown so vividly in the still face experiment the withdrawal of that gaze led to a complete unravelling and a turning away from the unresponsive face as though that would stop the desire for the gaze to return. In the adult version of this experiment, Abramović's onlookers ended up expressing a desire to kill her: if she were dead that would end their torment, their feeling of non-existence, and end their desire for a response.

The power of the female gaze in both these cases is apparent but what is also apparent is the desire/need to have a response and the difficulty for the audience is not so much the lack of response but the uncontrollable need to get it. It would be interesting to know if Abramović's performance would have had a different response if it had been a man's face that remained so emotionless, if the desire for a paternal gaze would have been as powerful as the need for a maternal gaze and the annihilation felt when this was not received. The withdrawal of the look elicited protest, aggression, and most importantly, as she described it, a 'madness' that took over the room. The real madness or overwhelming feeling was that of the need for the gaze; it is this that needs to be controlled but instead of this control being placed in the self, it becomes the woman who is seen to be the one in need of control, her presence that feels uncontrollable.

As Freud intimates in his paper '"Wild" psycho-analysis',[11] the introduction of a woman, her presence, will bring in something 'wild' to the psychoanalytic profession and can make a competent professional go awry. What Freud misplaces here is to whom the wildness belongs, attributing the wild feelings of the male professional to the female patient. It is of course these 'wild feelings' that men have towards women for which women traditionally have been held responsible. The most obvious example of this was (I use the past tense optimistically) the widely held belief that women were 'asking for it' if they went out wearing short skirts or clothing that exhibited the woman's body shape, the 'it' women were seen to be asking for being sex, and in the 'asking' being seen to be giving permission. The phrase 'asking for it' places all the responsibility with the woman; the man is not able to control his desire when confronted with what a woman may or may not be able to give him. The woman is seen as the master of desire, not the one who feels it and it is of course women who are perceived as the ones who can give or withhold the fulfilment of that desire, a grown-up echo of the infant's desire on the mother.

This desire is seen as so overwhelming, so bottomless, that the object of desire becomes the thing to be controlled rather than the desire itself. The 'wildness' to which Freud referred has to be tamed by taming the object, making sure that women have an authority placed over them. Women are punished for the desire that men have for them, almost unable to recover from the male trauma that they were once dependent on a woman, fully needing her, and yet the mother never fully needed or was dependent on him. As argued by Winnicott,[12] the inability to process this trauma and feel gratitude for the mother can lead to misogyny. It is not hard to imagine that one of the self-cures for this frustration and pain is in the denial of ever having needed a woman in the first place, blaming her for her inadequacy and not being totally dependent on him.

The way in which this control is asserted has taken many different forms, from the familiar direct role of patriarchy, ensuring that men have greater presence than women in prominent roles, to the more nuanced, such as controlling how women dress, titrating how much of the woman's physicality is allowed to be present. For women in psychoanalysis the dress code is sometimes explicit but more commonly implicitly set through the group uniform of wearing something that is considered to not be overtly sexual, not revealing too much skin, and 'neutral'. Women have been expected to wear something equivalent to the male dress code of 'smart casual'—trousers and a jacket. The inherent problem in this is that clothing is never 'neutral', indeed the choice for men of jacket and trousers communicates a formality, a certain background, and, more importantly, authority. A true women's equivalent does not exist as it would be mimicking the male template, so is intrinsically second place, aping the man's authority rather than having authority in her own right, collaborating with a history of male superiority in psychoanalysis.

As an example of the skill and precision of the child analyst Anna Freud, I was once told the story of an exchange that took place at her famous Wednesday clinics held at Maresfield Gardens, where she would sit on a chair whilst the candidates would sit on the floor awaiting comment from Freud's direct descendant. A candidate presented a session with a child patient. The details of the session were not recounted to me, however Anna Freud's comments were retold with joy and mystical admiration: 'Tell the mother to dress more modestly.' It was not clear from the anecdote if this had been a central theme to the child's analysis, but Anna Freud's criticism of an overly sexualised mother was clear. What was also clear from the anecdote was the unquestioning agreement that what women wear is powerful enough to drive their children into therapy and that Anna Freud had hit upon, with the precision of a surgeon's knife, that the physical manifestation of female sexuality was a cancerous tumour requiring removal. What was also unquestioned in this anecdote was the toxic perception of female sexuality that had been internalised by Anna Freud and also the candidates who were hanging on her every word. The message was clear: a woman can be maternal or sexual, but a bad mother is one who does not split off her sexuality from who she is as a mother; her sexuality is uncontrollable and therefore dangerous.

Through the control of what women wear, the physical presence of women can also be 'toned down', minimising the reality of her being a woman and not only a mother figure and therefore being in possession of the attributed 'wildness'. In much the same way as Anna Freud viewed the child's disturbance through the need for the mother to control her 'wildness', rather than addressing the child's 'wildness', it has been the same for women—if women's presence is contained then so will men's feelings be contained.

There is no need for the man to become distressed when she does not give him the response he desires. In this way the man can avoid the still face experiment and not have to confront his own need for maternal responsiveness and his original dependency on a woman. Which raises the question of who decided in psychoanalysis that women could only be 'maternal', nurturing figures and that female sexuality was to be excluded, unless of course it was to be pathologised. The origins of this may well lie in Freud but the subsequent repetition of this thought continues despite the many challenges to the contrary.

Within organisations versions of Tronick's 'still face' and Abramović's *Rhythm 0* are being enacted on a daily basis. It is a common joke of the woman in all-male meetings being spoken over, ignored, and then her ideas taken by one of the men and explained back to her as though it is a new idea that would be too complex for her to understand. The prevalence of this happening in reality in the workplace is not so humourous.[13,14] This turning away from the contents of the woman's mind and her presence is an iteration of the 'still face', where the baby's physical response to the responseless mother is to move his head away to keep the mother out of vision as her lack of response has to be negated, rendered invisible. In organisations when the woman is saying something that puts her in a position other than that of the nurturing mother, or is felt to be holding too much authority, the patriarchal response kicks in—they turn away from her, the injury to the sense of being and feelings of abandonment as the woman effectively steps out of her nurturing role and makes visible her own subjectivity is too much; *she* is too much.

Even in a field such as psychoanalysis that has had female analysts since shortly after its inception, and is predominantly female in membership, women have been turned away from, their role diminished, their physical life overlooked. This is evident from even a cursory look at the list of previous presidents of the International

Psychoanalytical Association, founded by Freud. Since it began in 1910 there have been twenty-five appointed presidents, all of whom were men until the first, and only, female president was appointed in 2017. Furthermore, of the twenty-five secretaries-general that have been in place, ten of these were women and of the eighteen treasurers in post only two of these have been women, the first being Phyllis Greenacre in 1957, the second being Nadine Levinson in 2003.[15] In the UK, in the original psychoanalytic establishment, The British Psychoanalytical Society, there is a slightly higher presence of women: of the thirty appointed presidents to date, eight have been women.[16] This history of inequality is sometimes speedily responded to with a reference to the 'controversial discussions'[17] as a reminder of the power of women within the psychoanalytic movement. The controversial discussions caused a split in the British Psychoanalytical Society as sides were drawn between those who supported Anna Freud and those who supported Melanie Klein. It is true that certain women have played prominent roles and made groundbreaking advances within psychoanalysis, but there is a risk in taking this as proof of a lack of systemic misogyny that would be equivalent to describing Margaret Thatcher's cabinet members as feminists, or the cliché of claiming to not be racist by virtue of having a best friend who is Black.

The International Psychoanalytical Society and the British Psychoanalytical Society are not alone in their lack of gender diversity. According to the UK Council for Psychotherapy (UKCP), in a member survey in 2016, 74% of members are female, 24% are male.[18] But a quick glance at former chairs of UKCP since it was formed in 1989 to date shows that out of the eleven chairs that have been in post, seven have been men, four were women,[19] and that there is clearly a disproportionate representation of women in the lead positions in these organisations. The disproportionate representation is, of course, not unusual but perhaps what is unusual is a lack of a well-publicised active plan to redress this or indeed to have an active discussion of psychoanalysis's own internalised misogyny that has permitted this to take place without question. It is as though the punishment and exclusion of women on the basis of their gender has been taken for granted or, worse still, it feels as if it has been let off the hook by virtue of having had some prominent female members—which paradoxically, instead of being reassuring that women are welcome as equals, serves as a reminder that women can be present, but it is still in men's gift to control what form that presence takes. This is illustrated by the advice given to me when taking over as Chair of a psychoanalytic organisation in 2019: a more senior male member of the psycho-analytic community confided in me to not 'fall into the trap of being a strident, strong woman or you won't get on well'.

CHAPTER THREE

Freud bingo

Whenever I attend a psychoanalysis conference there are a number of things that are always apparent upon entering the auditorium. The initial observation is the high proportion of women to men, followed by the clear lack of diversity—the room is literally whitewashed with white, middle-class people. Third is the dress code that seems to have been sent out in advance of the conference: oversized jewellery and crushed linen for women, suits or jeans and a jumper for men. There is a slight variation in the main three observations when the conference moves from a wider psychotherapeutic context to one which is more psychoanalytic, the striking difference being that the proportion of men seems to increase, as does the hierarchy of the more senior or prominent analysts sitting closer to the front, nearer to the speaker. The one variable that never changes is that regardless of the outnumbering of men to women, a number of men from the audience will always speak, more often than not being the first to contribute when the floor is opened for questions.

The most interesting and challenging moment at conferences is when the audience is allowed to speak. There is an etiquette by which the speaker is thanked for their 'rich' and 'illuminating' paper, even if most of the audience had fallen asleep, followed by what is best described as a battle of narcissism, whereby the attendee will 'pay back' for having had to endure listening to the speaker by then giving an uninvited mini paper of their own. Notably, often the most interesting interactions are usually when a one-line comment is given back, but sadly what more often happens is a sort of 'letting loose'. I often wonder if there is a sense of release for many of the therapists especially after having spent many hours alone with their patients, unobserved except *by* those patients. When the moment comes to be able to speak in front of a hundred-plus people, the moment is too irresistible to not hold forth and give what is often prefaced with 'my associations', many of which are thought-provoking, many are not. What is interesting in this is the inherent presumption that these 'associations' should be given and have merit in their own right.

At such moments I am intrigued as to what their patient's experience of them must be and if there is a distortion that occurs in being the psychotherapist in the psychotherapeutic relationship. For me it raises the risk that in therapy an echo chamber can be created, whereby the therapist has internalised so many core beliefs and thinking that as time progresses these become ossified and unbending to the therapeutic relationship, requiring the patient to contort and comply to that belief system. It seems that this system develops over time to become the therapist's formula of how to do therapy, an unconsciously developed defence mechanism to protect against the immediate threat of the uncertainty that is an intrinsic part of the psychoanalytic process. This uncertainty is part of the impossibility of exactly pinning down psychoanalysis and the unconscious in purely scientific terms. There is something unknown, and therefore unknowable, about a profession in which we are all involved.

The echo chamber seems to be a reflection of what happens in psychoanalytic conferences and writing. Theory and practice undoubtedly develop and move on but always return to drink from the same Freudian well, more often than not unquestioningly. It is always interesting when papers are presented as to how quickly and how often Freud is referenced in the text and, more importantly, why. Often there is a correlation between the increasing number of quotes from Freud and the increasing sense of restriction in thinking. It is a great paradox within psychoanalysis, and also a great loss, that the more an analyst wants to assert themselves within the profession the more they are expected to comply with a formula and choose their psychoanalytic tribe, whether that be Freudian, Contemporary Freudian, Kleinian, Winnicottian, Relational, Lacanian, etc.

The experience of sitting listening to several papers at psychoanalytic conferences can often be akin to being invited to watch people play a game for which you have to guess the rules. There is clearly an unspoken order as to where people sit and who they sit next to. When presenting a case study there is an importance attached to the frequency of sessions attended by the patient involved as an indication of the seriousness or depth of an analysis; there is authority assumed and given to certain attendees and certain presenters, and debates that rarely take place, such as a refusal of key Freudian concepts. This is by no means to say that there is no use or no interest in the papers presented, quite the opposite, but the question that resides is why, when there is 'rich' thought and material, does it get formatted in a way that means it has to tick the boxes of mentioning Freud a certain number of times, or going for a 'full house' of getting in 'primary narcissism', 'primal scene', and 'Oedipus complex'. But more concerning is the inclusion of phrases such as 'as we know from Freud' or 'Freud says' which gives the distinct tone of a cult but without acknowledging the harm that that can do.

The harm can be manifold. The obvious one, which unfortunately is familiar to most from childhood, is if you want to be part of 'our gang' then this is what we think, and failure to give up your own subjectivity and not adhere to one set of thinking is met with the pain of exclusion. (Most primary schools now forbid the forming of gangs or 'special groups' as they are seen as bullying.) But the more subtle implications can be far more detrimental. The taking for granted of Freudian theory inherently squashes down disagreement and creates an 'establishment' to be part of or not. In much the same way as Freud established his psychoanalytic movement initially by invitation only with the exclusion of people who disagreed with the theory, this tradition seems to have been continued. Given the splits that have occurred in psychoanalytic organisations, especially key ones such as the British Institute of Psychoanalysis,[1] it is perhaps not surprising that there would be a drive to create cohesion. As I was told by one analyst who had trained at the Institute in the years following the controversial discussions between Melanie Klein and Anna Freud, there was an incredibly unpleasant and bitter split between the three groups—the Freudians, Kleinians, and Independents—to the point where all necessary documentation such as notifications had to be printed in triplicate to be dispersed to each group; the hostility was so fierce that communication had almost entirely broken down between them. Given that this is still in living memory for some, the push for unity is understandable, but what one is being required to agree to for the sake of 'unity' is not.

Sitting and listening to papers with Freud's quotes given as statements of fact can evoke a range of feelings from one of boredom to coercion and in some cases like being a witness to something which has made you feel like you have 'sold out' for even being present. At times there can be a strong sense of being transported back to the nineteenth century where the neurologist Charcot would bring a hysterical women into the auditorium to be paraded in front of the male medical students. When presenting their work, some analysts use the guise of anonymity to give themselves permission to give a detailed description of every intimate detail of their patient. Frequently, the case of a modern-day hysterical woman is given, describing how she is given a new lease of life thanks to the 'enlightened' analyst telling her the error of her ways; and in the writing and presenting of such 'important work', the analyst overlooks that the patient coming to therapy should at the minimum expect privacy and ownership over the contents of her mind rather than it being exposed to anyone who can pay for a ticket.

The 'selling out' feeling becomes particularly personal when, as a woman, I contemplate what it is I am 'buying in to' when I accept Freudian theory unchallenged. When a woman is described as having 'oedipal issues' or her difficulties explained as being due to an 'unresolved Oedipus complex' without these terms being clearly defined, what am I being asked to accept? Is it that as a group we are all taking for granted an understanding of the Oedipus complex as described by Freud and therefore agreeing with misogyny? Apart from the instant feeling of having missed that day at school and therefore being put on the outside or made 'other' to the group, a group that has decided that psychoanalysis means agreeing to the Oedipus complex (not *all* psychoanalytic organisations formulate human development in this way), there is also the not so minor issue of the history that accompanies the use of these terms and what is conjured up by them. The full meaning of the Oedipus complex for women as described by Freud[2] meant that as a little girl, that girl would have realised that there was a lack in her due to not having a penis and if she wanted to successfully resolve this anxiety then she would resign herself to her inferior position; instead of longing for her own penis, she would content herself with that, one day, she would be able to marry a man and have a baby instead. Freud described this realisation of a lack of a penis as permanently marking the woman's sense of self, causing 'a scar, a sense of inferiority ... she begins to share the contempt felt by men for a sex which is the lesser in so important a respect'.[3]

Since Freud's description of the psychosexual development of women, there have been many who have contested this view, some also supplying alternate understandings of the Oedipus complex. His theory was quickly challenged by Karen Horney and Ernest Jones in the 1930s,[4,5] Clara Thompson in the 1950s,[6] Juliet Mitchell in the 1970s,[7] who redescribed the longing for a penis in more Lacanian terms, and more recently by Nancy Kulish and Deanna Holtzman[8] who reimagine the Oedipus complex incorporating women's experiences, replacing it for women as the 'Persephone complex'. Jessica Benjamin's[9] version of the Oedipus complex gives this development in the child's relationship with the parents the full emotional complexity in relational terms. There is a long history of people highlighting the flaws in Freud's construction of the Oedipus complex, the majority of which, unless they are variations on Freud's original theme have been dismissed, become sectioned off to a separate group within psychoanalysis, with some such as Horney even being banished from psychoanalytic institutions.[10] To be clear, the difficulty I am highlighting here is not so much with the theory, *though there is a lot of difficulty to be had with the theory*; the real issue lies in the use of these terms without acknowledging their history or indeed the full ramifications of the theory.

It is interesting why terms such as 'oedipal' and 'Oedipus complex' are not defined or redescribed in the papers being presented at conferences or in written papers; at best, the terms are glossed over as not being in 'the strictest Freudian sense', but any other sense is not given. There is the obvious answer to why these terms are used: it is a fundamental psychoanalytic concept. This in itself raises the question of if you have full knowledge of the concept and all that it encompasses then why would anyone not want to distance themselves from the misogyny inherent in their use? A possible clue to this is the original double bind set up by Freud in describing the Oedipus complex for women. If a woman argued against the Oedipus complex and the men defending it, then that would point to her being stuck in an unresolved Oedipus complex, not realising her need to submit to the greater knowledge of men.

Evidence of this double bind and the need for women to adhere to this area of Freudian metapsychology was apparent in the presentation of Freud's controversial paper, 'Some psychical consequences of the anatomical distinction between the sexes'.[11] In this paper he draws together other developments in his theory to provide a definitive picture of psychosexual development. Freud is also careful to reiterate an important point about his theory which is rarely currently commented on: his view of psychosexual development was based on male development and then it was assumed that female development would be the same. This was a fundamental flaw he was more than aware of but one that analysts seem to have let drop as not important enough to mention when quoting from Freud. To a current reader, or one not familiar with Freud, there are some alarming conclusions arrived at in the paper which depict women as inferior, jealousy-driven, with poor judgement, stating that:

> We must not allow ourselves to be deflected from such conclusions by the denials of the feminists, who are anxious to force us to regard the two sexes as completely equal in position and worth. (p. 258)

Due to ill health, Freud was unable to present this paper in person to The Homburg International Psychoanalytic Congress, so instead asked his daughter, Anna Freud, to present the paper.[12] It seems extraordinarily humiliating for a woman to be asked to do this, especially his daughter, but in one fell swoop Freud made it clear that for any woman to join the psychoanalytic society, she must accept her place or be pathologised.

It is this same message that reverberates whenever a Freud quote is given as a law. After all, if one accepts one Freud quote without challenge or a new definition being given, isn't one accepting then the value of any quote as long as it comes from Freud? The more nuanced tone in the reciting of Freud quotes is that you must adhere and pay due respect or you are on the outside, a not good enough member of the psychoanalytic community. The real problem arises when one considers what is constituting 'not good enough', which in Freud's view was quite clearly women. The need to quote Freud in papers, often repeatedly, seems to be a need for authority or 'gravitas'; the more Freud is mentioned or included without contest, the closer the author of the paper gets to Freud, declaring his/her loyalty to Freudian doctrine. What is curious is the need to continue the identification and to continue the feeling of the 'boys club' in which psychoanalysis was founded. What is more curious is that this misogynistic identification is blatantly apparent but in a field where the main interest of the day is understanding unconscious processes, this particular process advances unhindered.

As mentioned above, one reason for the continued association with a misogynistic theory that takes male development as the 'norm' is that the identification with Freud and the authority placed in him supersedes all other needs. The continued faith in Freud provides a defensive barrier against the critics of psychoanalysis. In a world in which great store is set by evidence-based practice, and there is a great divergence of viewpoints about what 'works' in psychoanalysis and what even the 'outcome' should be, there is an obvious benefit in reifying Freud at all costs, even if one of these includes having to submit to a male-dominated theory. However, this need to defend also points to an insecurity. As Freud himself so brilliantly uncovered, defences are there to protect a vulnerability or fragility in the self; perhaps it is this basic but crucial flaw of repeating a theory built on crumbling foundations without acknowledging this and correcting the misogynistic theory that rattles the defences of the psychoanalytic community. There is something shameful in the history of psychoanalysis which needs to be acknowledged. But it seems that there is a paralysis in this move to acknowledgement, as the real shame is in the fact that the misogyny is not historical, it is present and holds back true development. In much the same way as trauma gets stuck and there is a need to repeat, to go back to the scene of the crime to try and rework the event to get a better outcome, it feels that psychoanalysis is caught in that same loop of repetition, too afraid to allow itself to be properly analysed and live with that part of itself that has caused further trauma by its actions not only to women but also to marginalised groups.

It is, of course, also possible that the unconscious process of adhering to misogyny in the repetition of quoting Freud as a piece of law is not such an unconscious process. The boys' club of psychoanalysis certainly maintains the benefits of white middle-class male privilege and feeds into well-proven gender biases such as caring being an attribute of women whilst leadership qualities pertain to men.[13] As was said to me on several occasions by a senior male analyst during my training as an attachment-based psychoanalytic psychotherapist, 'Bowlby said that psychotherapy was women's work', the implication being that the intellectual rigour of theory was men's work. Of course, what was more fascinating to me was why this analyst would feel the need to say this. The misogyny of the comment was not lost on me, nor the reminder to pay respect to my 'male elders' and keep to my place. The analyst expected me to swallow the comment as a truth in much the same way as Freud quotes are given to remind everyone of the rules of play.

It is exactly these implicit 'rules of play' that have sustained the continuation of the misogyny inherent in psychoanalysis. I have been part of different groups reading, studying, and teaching Freud over many years. When I have taught Freud seminars to different groups, I would sometimes share with the group that when I first started reading Freud, I could draw a map to show the different places around London where I have fallen asleep with a Freud paper in my hand. My point was that it can be hard and off-putting to read Freud initially but there is much to be gained from the struggle. He is known for provoking strong reactions but there is a commonality in the reactions that have emerged over time. In all the groups I have been a part of, a divide has taken place between those who 'get' Freud and those who do not, often causing a state of confusion and exasperation for the latter. It was not until I was in a much larger group studying Freud that the divide became more apparent; rarely did the men find Freud off-putting or difficult to read, whilst the women would huddle to share notes and become anxious to make sense of the readings. It was at this point that it became apparent to me that I struggled with Freud because it was never written for me, it was written by a man for men. The best I could hope for was to eavesdrop on the proceedings whilst it was more than instinctive for men to understand them. My real problem was that I had to find out that 'rule of play' for myself, it was never presented as an inherent bias in understanding Freud, placing the difficulty with the reader rather than the writer.

Challenging Freud's view of psychosexual development was initially quashed and put into the bracket of insubordination or betrayal.[14] As time has gone on and the challenges continued, they either disappeared or were put into another bracket of 'feminist psychoanalysis'. This is not to say that Freud's original theory has been stuck to without change, it is more that the Oedipus complex and the position of women within Freud's writing is often glossed over.

There is often an assumed given that the term is used with the idea of female submission being outdated, but it is rarely qualified as to what that updated version is or the redescription does little to improve the original placing of women. In *Seeing and Being Seen* by John Steiner,[15] a well-known and often cited book, his new version of the Oedipus complex is the playing out of the 'feminine' and 'masculine' positions, the feminine being the one who receives and takes in goodness, the masculine being the aggressive, active position. Whilst the feminine position is not seen as exclusively pertaining to women nor the masculine as exclusively pertaining to men, the language used is, and furthers, the stereotype in using this language. If a woman wants to be a woman, then by these terms she needs to take in goodness, be passive, or risk being too much like a man. The term used in this way has been misappropriated, owned by a man to apply a man-made theory to women.

The outdated nature of these terms is unavoidably striking if they are taken out of their own realm and compared to contemporary culture. There have been different receptions to the song 'WAP' ('Wet Ass Pussy') by Cardi B, featuring Megan Thee Stallion, which entered the American charts at number one in 2020 and was also number one in several other countries. The reception of the song became a story in its own right when an American political commentator, Ben Shapiro, criticised the song for its overt sexual references and depiction of women, for which he was widely ridiculed. But what was obvious from the lyrics is that the two women who wrote and performed the song had clear demands about sex. They were clear about what they wanted to 'give' and what they wanted to do whilst 'receiving' to make it more enjoyable for themselves, rather than the usual perspective of women's sexuality being about what the woman can do to please the man. The song was widely lauded for its current attitude to female sexuality which is in stark contrast to that of Steiner's updated 'feminine position'. From a Cardi B perspective the idea of a woman being there to be submissive and passively receive what she is given would have nothing to do with being feminine or a woman. The question then surely has to be why psychoanalysis so far has not stepped outside of its comfort zone and addressed its own insecurity? Rather than hiving off gender and sexual equality as a specialist subject, psychoanalysis needs to address its own misogyny and the continued impact it has not only on limiting women but also the value of psychoanalysis.

CHAPTER FOUR

The misogynistic introject—a case study

The English psychoanalyst Bion famously wrote that the analyst should enter a session with a patient without memory or desire: 'Memory is always misleading as a record of fact ... Desires interfere, by absence of mind when observation is essential'.[1] When training as a therapist, this quote is often mentioned as an 'in joke' to calm anxieties about not being able to remember theoretical points or feeling insecure about not knowing enough to help the person sitting opposite you in a consulting room. What Bion was alluding to was his much more complex ideas about what gets in the way of the more important work happening in analysis.

This 'in joke' for trainees helps soothe anxieties because it gently reminds the trainee that, in order to be at the point of being in a consulting room with their first patient, the trainee has already undertaken a significant amount of training in a psychoanalytic or psychotherapeutic institution. This training includes reading and writing about psychoanalysis, attending seminars being given by more senior analysts, the trainee analyst's own analysis and supervision. All of which, of course, is determined by the theoretical orientation of the training institution, which in itself decides the theoretical emphasis and understanding of what it means to be a person.

It is the point at which a therapist sits down with their patient in a consulting room that this training comes to life. It is also the point at which the inherent misogyny in psychoanalysis should be of importance to anyone who is involved in any way with psychoanalysis.

The following case study of a mother and daughter who are repeatedly met with, and failed by, a rigid theoretical understanding of mothers and their children illustrates the corrosive impact of the way women have been conceptualised in psychoanalysis. The loss is not just to the restrictive thinking in the discipline but there is also a real impact on those families who need support.

A woman in her early thirties sought help due to an ongoing feeling of anxiety and inadequacy following the birth of her first child. The first five months of her baby's life had presented significant challenges to the new parents, they had had little if no experience of newborns, there were no nearby grandparents to offer support, and they were the first of their friendship group to have a baby.

Following the first few days after returning home from hospital, the parents had found it increasingly difficult to settle their baby to sleep in her Moses basket. The baby woke frequently during the night to breastfeed, often then vomiting the feed back, only for the process to be started again. On some nights the baby would wake every half hour, feed, fall asleep whilst breastfeeding and then wake, vomit, and want to feed again. The parents had worked out a system between them where for the first month the father stayed awake cradling the baby, rocking her to sleep in his arms, then when she would wake, take her to the mother to feed and then leave the mother to return to sleep and get some rest. The mother would then take over the care of the baby during the day. They were both exhausted but when the mother took the baby to the GP to discuss the feeding problems, the GP suggested trying to wind the baby more after feeding, which the mother was already doing, and promised the mother that when the baby reached six weeks old things would settle down.

Six weeks came and went, with little change except the parents had worked out that if they carefully positioned rolled-up blankets either side of the baby and at the bottom of her feet, she would settle for short naps in the Moses basket. The parents read several parenting manuals, and the mother talked to other new mothers at baby groups, mining them for information as to how she could help her baby sleep more. The mother also discovered a new term for babies that fed and slept well, when a health visitor asked her if her baby was a 'good baby'. The mother, confused by the question, replied that her baby was lovely, it had not occurred to her that a baby could be 'bad', especially for not being able to sleep. She wondered if, in fact, the term was really meant to be a description of the mother and realised that she would have placed herself in the 'bad' category, especially as she could not feed her baby successfully nor settle her to sleep.

When the baby was five months old the mother self-referred to a locally well-known baby and child psychotherapy clinic. The mother and baby met with a therapist, the mother explained her concerns—she was breastfeeding, her baby frequently vomited in the night, at most her baby would sleep for three hours, naps in the day meant that the mother would continuously walk around the park as the movement was the only way to get her baby off to sleep other than falling asleep on the breast as she fed. On days when the mother was especially exhausted, she would let her baby fall asleep whilst feeding and the mother would then lie down on the sofa with the baby asleep on the mother's chest, nuzzled into her. This concerned the mother as she felt guilty because this was against all the medical guidance for how a baby should sleep. The therapist asked how the mother was going to have her daily nap when she went back to work; the mother replied that she had not worked it out yet. But what was really pressing for the mother was that she wanted the therapist to give her guidance on how she could get her baby to sleep in a cot. The baby now filled the Moses basket, which the baby seemed to enjoy, snuggling into the sides of the basket as she settled to sleep. The parents had moved the basket to inside the cot as a sort of transition but every time the mother tried to move the baby into the cot, she was unable to settle and would cry, meaning that no one got any sleep. The therapist commented that it was difficult for a mother and baby to separate and asked what the baby was going to do when she was eighteen years old, 'Put her legs through the Moses basket?' The mother went once more to see the therapist but, feeling more resourceless when she left the session than when she arrived, the parents agreed that they would try and work it out for themselves.

By the time the child was four years old the parents had another two children. The second child would amaze the parents at her ability to settle off to sleep by herself in her cot, sleeping up to six hours a night after being breastfed. The parents noticed the difference in the early few weeks of each of their children and with more conversations with different parents, realised that their first baby had suffered from severe reflux, meaning she was unable to hold the feeds of milk or lie down flat in a Moses basket without it causing her pain. The mother had talked about the baby's symptoms to her GP and the therapist, both of whom had commented on how much mothers worry. The mother's anger at the lack of help for her child was translated into a sense of guilt, blaming herself for not knowing or not fighting hard enough to get her child help, her confidence in her own ability as a mother increasingly diminished.

Six months after her eldest child had started primary school, the mother asked her new GP to refer her for therapy. The mother had had a useful experience of therapy in her twenties following a bereavement and felt that she needed help with the anxieties she was having about her children and unrelenting feelings of not being 'good enough' which would stop her from falling asleep at night. The mother started weekly therapy for a year. The main theme of the work was the mother's concern with her eldest child's primary school. Although the parents had actively sought out this highly regarded school for their child to attend, the reality was that their daughter was immensely unhappy going into school each morning. The mother found the school to be cold and not especially caring, with the exception of certain staff, but more importantly what was distressing for the mother was that her child would cry every morning before being dropped off at class, clinging on to the mother's arm. The four-year-old had also developed a bald patch at the side of her head where she would anxiously twizzle her hair all day and she would come out of school with the cuffs of her cardigan wringing wet and in tatters where she would chew on them whilst sitting in class. By the second term the parents had met with the head teacher who assured them that their child was 'very quiet' but happy when in school; she frequently asked the teacher throughout the day when it would be time to go home, but the head teacher considered this not unusual and said that she could be easily distracted on to something else.

During the therapy sessions the mother would often be upset, feeling that she had failed her daughter and worried if she would be able to do better for her other two children. The mother would often try to explain to the therapist that due to her own childhood she had the photo negatives of how not to raise a child, but lacked the colour photograph of what a happy childhood would look like, not knowing what was normal for a child going to school or what a mother should do. The therapist was moved by the mother, and in a very understanding and caring tone would redescribe the mother's anxieties about the school as being her projections of her own fears about herself. She would explain that in much the same way as the mother did not feel that she knew how to bring up a child, it was difficult for the mother to trust that the school would know how to care for a child and therefore the mother would experience them as cold and uncaring. Some time was also spent exploring the mother's apparent anxiety about separation as the therapist felt this was key to the distress she was experiencing, that the daughter had clearly picked up on this anxiety and was now acting it out in school. The therapist encouraged the mother to think about the school as not such a harsh place, it could even be 'good enough' and that this would help the child to feel more confident going to school. The mother would often struggle with this idea as she had been excited and keen for her child to make this significant step in going to school. She knew she would miss her child when she was there, but the mother had been used to her daughter going to nursery and also had her daughter's two younger siblings to look after. When this was voiced, the therapist would comment that it was hard for the mother to fully acknowledge the pain of separation.

In the winter of the daughter's third year at school, she had become more settled. She was still ambivalent about being dropped off but as long as her usual 'drop off' routine had taken place and she knew what classes were planned for the day she would be less anxious. The parents had also developed a strictly adhered-to routine in the mornings which would help their daughter feel more relaxed and they had a game that they would play every morning without fail on the way to school. The parents knew that if the routine or game changed their daughter would become anxious and withdrawn. Towards the end of term there was an incident in the classroom which left the child feeling physically trapped and unable to escape from school. The fear about going to school, which the child was just about managing to contain, exploded with even the thought of going to school causing the child to sob, curling up into the foetal position and hiding herself under a blanket.

The parents worked with a psychologist to develop a plan to get the daughter on to the school grounds—at this point even driving near the school would trigger the child to cry uncontrollably—until eventually after several months the daughter was able to go into school and stay in class as long as her mother or father stayed at an agreed place in the school building. The mother and father spent considerable time reading and researching ways to help their daughter. The mother attended a conference for teachers, psychologists, and child psychotherapists on the subject of school anxiety and phobia. During the break the mother approached one of the speakers, a psychotherapist, and gave a brief outline of the incident at school, that her child had always been anxious going to school, that the child needed routine at home and in school, and that she was now only able to be in school if one of the parents were present. The mother did not reveal that it was her child for fear that the psychotherapist might not give a full answer. The therapist explained that for any child to be anxious about school, they had 'clearly not taken in enough of the mother into their ego'. The mother asked why this might be as the child's mother had always been present, very much loved the child, and enjoyed the time at home playing and looking after the child and her two siblings. The therapist replied that as a professional it is often so hard to know from the outside, but that without doubt something must have happened with the mother. At this point the mother, still wanting an answer to help her child, asked that if that were not the case and that if you knew there had not been any trauma at home that would cause the anxiety, what could it be? She then told the therapist that she knew the case well as it was her child.

The therapist then politely excused herself as she needed to prepare for the next presentation.

Over the next two years the daughter was referred to different professionals by other professionals, including education psychologists, an inclusion specialist, systemic psychotherapist, cognitive behavioural therapy (CBT) therapist, and a child analyst who was also trained in eye movement desensitization and reprocessing (EMDR)—a therapy treatment for trauma. The working premise for all of these professionals was that the parents, especially the mother, needed to be less involved and had not separated enough from their child. The inclusion specialist outlined that the daughter had to be in school full-time as 'it was the best place for children rather than being at home' and recommended a further referral to psychiatry for her to be medicated so that she attended school. The professionals involved would often miss, until it was brought to their attention by the mother, that there were two other children in the family, the father worked full-time and the mother worked part-time, so the parents were also keen for their child to be in school full-time and without them being present at school.

At the mother's suggestion, the psychotherapy clinic to which the daughter had been referred arranged for the daughter, accompanied by the mother, to meet with the child analyst to try using EMDR as this was a highly recommended treatment for trauma. The mother hoped that it might unlock the trauma the child experienced at school where she had felt trapped but had never been able to talk to the parents about the incident. It was also hoped that the physical activity of EMDR might be of more interest to the daughter (the patient is asked to squeeze something in their hand) especially as the meeting with the CBT therapist had been unsuccessful. The CBT therapist had repeatedly suggested throughout the session for the mother to leave the room, despite this being the first time the child, by this time eight years old, had been in the building and was the first time meeting the therapist, resulting in the child collapsing in tears and clinging to the mother.

The initial stages of the EMDR session had gone well but the child soon became withdrawn and began to stare down at her feet. The analyst continued talking to the mother and daughter as the child looked increasingly uncomfortable, repeatedly digging her shoe in to the floor and pinching her fingers. The mother explained to the analyst that the daughter was showing that she needed to leave as the session had become too much for her. The mother, from previous experience, was more than aware that if there were to be any hope of her daughter returning for another session, they would need to leave as soon as possible. At this point the analyst suggested to the mother that it was she, the mother, who needed to come to therapy and then turned to the daughter, thanking her for coming and told her that she did not think that 'this' was her fault but that it was 'the family's fault'.

It is of note that this was the first meeting, the analyst had not met the father, nor did she suggest that the father also be in therapy. The analyst's diagnosis was also not based on an in-depth conversation with the mother. If she had done this, the analyst might have discovered that the mother had already by this time found a psychotherapist whom she was seeing on a regular basis to help her manage the stress and at times trauma of trying to find support for her daughter.

The mother, having some knowledge of autism, had wondered if her child's anxiety, reluctance in managing change, and becoming unsettled when routines were changed was due to autism, but was reluctant for her child to be given a 'label'. As time progressed and there were noticeable differences in her daughter's communication style to those of her peers, differences that both parents actually preferred and valued, the mother asked the therapist managing her daughter's case to refer her for an autism assessment so that it could be ruled out. As several months passed with no appointment offered, the mother assumed this was due to a waiting list and asked the therapist to check how far down they were on the list for assessment, at which point the therapist said that she had 'lost' the form and would fill out another. More months passed and eventually the daughter was offered an appointment with a psychiatrist and the systemic therapist to assess if she should be referred for assessment. The mother asked if the assessment could take place at her child's school as it was extremely likely that meeting in a new room in a strange building with two strangers would cause her daughter to 'shutdown' and become upset, but was told that the assessment could only take place at the therapy centre and that 'most children usually manage with this'. At the meeting the child said 'hello' and after a few moments put her head down, staring at her hands, occasionally looking at the door, not responding to questions from the psychiatrist; when she began to cry and was unable to be soothed, the parents suggested they end the assessment.

The week following the assessment the parents met with the psychiatrist and the systemic therapist. The psychiatrist conveyed her understanding at the parents' concern about their daughter as she could see how unable the child was to manage the social interaction and her clear distress. The parents expressed their lack of surprise as this had happened before with the CBT therapist, the analyst practicing EMDR, and the educational psychologist. The psychiatrist asked the parents what they wanted 'to do' about their daughter. The mother's head dropped in despair, the otherwise even-tempered father looked at the mother and angrily replied that if he had broken his leg and gone to an emergency department, he would not expect the doctor to ask him what he should do. The father then directly said that they and their service was not good enough, that they were failing a child who was suffering. Very shortly following the meeting the psychiatrist wrote a full report, recommending the child for an autism assessment.

The mother's story and experience of seeking help for her child is unfortunately not remarkable. There are many mothers of children who have additional support needs or who do not fit into the normal trend of schooling and education who are met with the same difficulties and the same dismissive attitude from the professionals they approach for help. The one theme that is repeated when one talks to these mothers is not just that they are perceived as being over-anxious, narcissistic, or entitled—thinking that their child deserves special treatment. It is that the professional knows better than the mother.

Why this assumption exists could be for many reasons, not least of all the obvious in that the mother is seeking advice and knowledge from that professional, but there seems to be something more fundamental at play. As the exchange between this mother and the GP demonstrates, when the mother is concerned about the newborn's feeding pattern, the GP quickly dismisses this as 'maternal anxiety'. The GP assumed that the woman and her ability to process her anxiety separately to her feeling that there is something wrong with the baby's feeding pattern or her ability to understand a baby, especially her *own* baby, is immediately lessened due to the fact that she *is* the mother. The same assumption is repeated throughout the mother's encounters with other professionals; at each turn her knowledge of her child is dismissed and undervalued because she *is* the mother rather than the obvious that would be expected that the person with the best knowledge, experience, and best placed to help the professional understand the child would *be* the mother.

The acknowledgement of the importance of the mother would also accept that mothers have intimate knowledge of their babies and knowledge that cannot be learnt or acquired unless the important work of mothering is done. Of course, that acknowledgement in its own right would mean an acceptance that being a mother is an important job in the first place and that all of us as newborns are dependent on that work, indeed dependent on women full stop to give birth to the baby. Winnicott described this fear of dependency as 'the fear of woman',[2] something that we all have to come to terms with and acknowledge:

> The root of this fear of woman is known. It is related to the fact that in the early history of every individual … there is a debt to a woman—the woman who was devoted to that individual as an infant, and whose devotion was absolutely essential for that individual's healthy development. (p. 252)

Winnicott also attributes this fundamental fear as 'responsible for the immense amount of cruelty to women, which can be found in customs that are accepted by almost all civilisations' (p. 252). This theory was used by Winnicott to explain a fear of dominance that would continue throughout the person's life if this fundamental reliance on a woman was not recognised. This fear of dominance in men due to women being able to give birth and being perceived as having the upper hand in this respect was first formulated by Karen Horney in 1926 in 'The flight from womanhood: the masculinity-complex in women as viewed by men and women'.[3] This was her response to Freud's theory of penis envy[4] which was never accepted by Freud and generally dismissed, only to be taken up much later and accepted once developed by a man, Winnicott.

This 'fear', as described by Winnicott, can be seen in patriarchal societies in general but more significantly it is also played out in the medical and psychoanalytic treatment of the mother as she repeatedly attempts to get help for her child. Through all the professionals that this mother meets there is a flow of an unconscious belief of the problem always lying with the mother. The real concern in this is the speed with which this belief becomes apparent; barely any time is given to understand *this* mother before a general principle about all mothers is applied. This starts with the

GP placing the newborn's health problems in the anxious psyche of the mother, to the child analyst who almost instantly diagnoses the child's response as due to the mother's need for help via therapy. This unconscious flow is even more startling when one considers that the father was actively involved in the care of the daughter and had been since birth, yet there is no questioning of his influence on the child or that as the child analyst describes, 'the fault', if there were one, may lie with the father. However, what is more devastating in this mother and baby's experience is the inability for any of the professionals to take the mother's concerns seriously; instead her judgement is repeatedly questioned, ignored, or worse, pathologised.

In several encounters with different psychotherapists who were more convinced of their own judgement about the woman's anxiety rather than even momentarily entertaining that the child might have additional support needs, or that the mother's anxiety might be due to the difficulties her child was encountering rather than vice versa, there was a paralysis in thinking. It is not surprising that the mother felt less skilled after leaving the first psychotherapist when her child was a baby. The mother already had a harsh internal voice that was critical of her efforts as a mother which then became externalised via the psychotherapist. At no point were the mother's concerns taken seriously: the therapist, if not directly belittling the mother's worries, would take a more stereotypically patriarchal position of 'settling down' the anxious woman.

The therapist could have engaged with why the mother felt so resourceless and unable to move her baby from the Moses basket to the cot. In fact, the therapist could have had many different thoughts, but the presumption was made that the mother did not have the skills. The therapist became the mother's harsh internal voice, enacting the mother's worst fears that the baby was not progressing due to her inadequacies. The therapist seemed to be remarkably unaware of what was being acted out by both the mother and herself; she voiced the critical patriarchal attitude typical towards women who struggle as new mothers, undermining the woman and portraying the skills of being a mother as being obvious, straightforward, and somehow innate. The mother, as with most women, was already aware due to her own internalised misogyny that struggling as a mother somehow made her 'less than' so would readily agree with the therapist's opinion and feel the hopelessness of her inadequacy.

But the catch in all of this is that a mother and baby psychotherapy clinic should be the one place where this misogyny is owned and understood, instead of being reinforced through the unquestioned misogyny in psychoanalysis that also expects the work of mothering to be innate or the mother is at fault. The baseline presumption of the mother's fault excludes all other curiosity as to what might also be happening with the baby; the strength of the presumption means thinking is repeatedly bounced back to what becomes the only explanation, the deficits in the mother.

The mother's position presents the no-win situation for all mothers: if the mother is concerned and seeking help then she is seen as over-involved, anxious, merged with the baby; if she does not act quickly enough then she is selfish, negligent, self-involved; if she does not complain or voice concerns about her baby then she is taken for granted as doing an easy job that is innate for women.

The mother told me that when there was an 'important' meeting she would ensure that her husband left work so that he could also attend as she knew that they would then be taken more seriously. The mother's experience of how she was treated, and more importantly how the parents would then be treated, seemed to accurately mark this unconscious flow; the maternal witness could not be trusted, was unreliable, what carried much more weight was the opinion of the father. However, in this case it was not just a benign form of sexism at work (if sexism can ever be benign): the conviction within the psychoanalytic thinking of the psychotherapists and psychoanalysts led to the mother effectively being gaslighted into thinking that the child's difficulties were her fault. In much the same way as Freud[5] described dreams as the 'royal road to a knowledge of the unconscious', it seems that there is a psychoanalytic royal road that leads all child difficulties exclusively back to the mother.

There is an inherent gender bias in psychoanalysis that is blatantly apparent in a cursory reading of any of the key writers—Freud, Winnicott, Klein, Bion, Anna Freud—in which the main writing, whilst being about the individual, is organised around the care that is given by the mother. Even in later writings and divergences such as that with Bowlby and attachment theory, despite Bowlby asserting that what he was describing was about the mother or mother substitute, he repeatedly uses only the term 'mother'. There is a noticeable absence of the father figure or the impact the father may have on the child; all neuroses in later life are fed back to one source, the mother. This is not to deny the importance that primary carers have on the child, but what is clearly denied when blame is being apportioned for later disturbances in psychic development, is the role of anyone other than the mother. The mother for psychoanalysis seems to have occupied an accepted place of being the one who is taken for granted when she gets it right and is vilified when she does not. It seems that this misogyny towards women has gone by in psychoanalysis not without question but has been unconsciously swallowed and incorporated into the role of the psychoanalyst.

The not-so-subtle scapegoating of women is not unusual in a patriarchal society, however what is unusual, if not shocking, is that this scapegoating can so directly take place in psychoanalysis. After all, psychoanalysis is a discipline which sets out to explore the unconscious processes and has a strong presence of women, but misogyny has found not only a hiding place but one that is in plain sight. It seems that the psychoanalytic idea of introjection, whereby other people's beliefs are taken in to become part of one-self, describes what has happened to psychoanalysis, in that the misogynistic wishes of the forefathers have been internalised by the psychoanalyst as a misogynistic introject.

In much the same way as there was no point of reflection in the mother and infant's story above, that considered that perhaps the mother's concerns were valid and not a by-product of the mother's pathology, there is an apparent starting point that mothers are guilty until proven innocent. This starting point of wrongly blaming mothers has a long-standing history in psychoanalysis from which there does not seem to be any learning or reparation. This is particularly stark in the history of autism where the psychiatrist Kanner, in 1943,[6] described the coldness of *parents* towards their children causing autism, however it was the psychoanalyst Bettelheim who focused in on the mother, promoting the label 'refrigerator *mother*' and seeing mothers as the main cause of their child's 'disorder'.[7] The blaming of parents became transparently entrenched in psychoanalysis by Frances Tustin who had dedicated most of her career to working with children with autism and who had given significant insights into the neurodivergent thinking of people with autism. In 1994, even against a backdrop of a vehement rejection of the idea of 'refrigerator mothers' and an expansion of research into the different possible biological, genetic, and psychological causes of autism, she still maintained that the cause lay with the interplay of a depressed mother with an infant with a 'constitutional vulnerability'. Tustin depicts mothers of autistic infants as 'clinging to her baby for comfort and support' who have 'blacked out the baby's separate active existence' (p. 107).[8]

It is painful to even imagine how this mother and child's experience might have been different if the underlying thought had been one of expecting the mother to be the expert and of being capable of being in tune with her daughter. If the mother had been taken as a reliable witness, it might have been quickly seen that the mother was capable of settling a baby to sleep, but that *her* baby was not able to settle to sleep. The baby might have got attention for a physical problem causing her feeding and sleeping problems. The various early markers for autism, such as the difficulty in the transition from home to school, the anxiety the child experienced in repeatedly asking when it was time to go home, chewing through her sleeve, and repetitively playing with her hair causing a bald patch, could have been recognised and the family been given the support they needed. When the child started school, if the mother had seen a psychoanalyst who had not internalised a psychoanalytic doctrine that considered the child's anxiety as being caused by an overanxious mother, then the analyst might have been able to genuinely listen to the mother and consider that the school was not 'good enough', it was not giving the child the support she needed.

The misogyny inherent in psychoanalytic training is teaching analysts to take mothers as unreliable narrators of their own and their children's stories. It would be interesting to have a clear view on what kind of narrator or witness fathers are taken to be, but unfortunately the literature is somewhat lacking. This lack in itself points to the ease with which psychoanalysis has comforted itself with women as the scapegoat, and no further investigation has been seen to be needed. It has been over sixty years since Winnicott wrote his paper, 'Primary maternal preoccupation',[9] setting out the sensitivity and attention of the mother to her newborn baby, but there has so far been no reply in terms of an exploration of primary paternal preoccupation, either about its presence or absence or what 'normal' paternal preoccupation would look like. There is an intriguing gap in interest in describing what normal father–child development should look like, perhaps because the men who might lead that research already have an awareness of how restrictive that would be.

This misogynistic introject has passed through generations of psychoanalysts via seminars, the training analysis, and supervision. It engenders entitlement in male psychoanalysts and shame and otherness in female psychoanalysts. This misogyny is transmitted and acted on without question, stifling thinking. It was of note that the final driver in the mother's search for help with her daughter was when the father became angry with the psychiatrist and the systemic therapist, his naming of their service as 'not being good enough'. In a heady combination of the misogynistic introject in both the psychiatrist and psychotherapist accepting his male entitlement and resonating with the women analysts' misogynistic introject of not being good enough, his view was accepted without being pathologised. Despite the mother's numerous attempts at trying to get support for her daughter, the blame was always pushed back on to the mother as being due to her anxiety. The more important question was never asked as to if the mother had reason to be anxious. Instead of curiosity about the mother and child, well-worn psychoanalytic tropes were applied that missed the point.

This mother and child's experiences highlight the many errors not just of a misogynistic view but of an unrecognised and institutionalised misogynistic view within psychoanalysis. This is not to say that the psychoanalytic approach is of no use, it is the opposite, but there is need for a genuinely controversial discussion where psychoanalysis can be reimagined as not coming from a place embedded in defensive misogyny and stops gaslighting itself.

CHAPTER FIVE

The missing period
in psychoanalysis

A bove Freud's couch at Maresfield Gardens in London is
a homage to the origins of the staging of his consulting
room. A picture hangs on the wall of the French neurologist Charcot giving one of his famous lectures in his lion's den at
Salpêtrière Hospital.[1] In the painting Charcot takes centre stage,
formally dressed. He stands addressing his all-male audience
whilst next to him is his medical specimen—a woman being supported to stand by another man; she reclines backwards in a semi-
conscious state. The woman's dress has been taken off to the waist,
her corseted undergarments exposed revealing her bare shoulders
and chest, her breasts just covered by her undershirt. The female
exhibit's clothes are in stark contrast to the formality of the men
surrounding her and the two female staff standing behind her. The
male audience look on engrossed, clamouring forward to watch
the unfolding drama.

Charcot's exposition of these hysterical women was a catalyst of Freud's own exploration of the 'mad' women, so troubled by their own uteruses (hysteria coming from the Greek word for uterus—*hystera*),[2] that they had lost their minds—their ticks, stammers, paralysis being the performance art of the neurosis caused by their own female anatomy. In Freud's attempts to cure these women, he saw that there was more than 'madness', there was a cause for this madness—a disturbance in what he called their 'psychosexual' development. In order to resolve the need for the physical communication of their neurosis, Freud asked these women to lie on his couch and talk to him whilst he delved into their psyche, unravelling what was in the minds of these women and the conflict and tension that was being caused by their sexual desires.

Long before Freud, and continued into the time of Freud's medical training, physicians working with hysterical women had attempted to cure their symptoms through the use of machines applied to the women's genitals to bring about orgasm thereby releasing tension.[3] Freud abandoned the physicality of women, seeing the best route of understanding women as being through their minds, the uterus itself being seen primarily as an empty receptacle waiting to be filled and not much more. In the move to treating his patients through words rather than touch, Freud still very much had the physical body in mind describing the ego as 'first and foremost a body ego' as it is 'ultimately derived from bodily sensations'.[4] Unfortunately, Freud then fell into the trap that modern medicine still continues, of basing theories on the male body[5] rather than the fuller picture of what the female body might mean. Freud abandoned the physicality of what made women different, in a way that threw the baby out with the bathwater not because the baby was not valuable but because that particular baby for Freud, by his own admission, was too different to be understood.[6,7]

In 1975 Carolee Schneemann performed *Interior Scroll* at *Women Here and Now*[8] in which she placed her body and, most importantly, her uterus at centre stage. Wearing nothing except a white apron, she entered the room, stood up on a table and daubed herself in black paint. Schneemann's self-exhibition could not be more different from the woman on Charcot's stage where the medical specimen's sexuality is alluded to by her state of semi-undress, her chest partly exposed, the viewer becoming as voyeuristic as the all-male audience leaning forward to see more of the semi-conscious woman. In *Interior Scroll*, Schneemann did not allude to her sexuality but stated it as a matter of fact. Once on the table, standing naked, she proceeded to unfurl paper from her vagina, reading aloud the words she had written on the scroll. The words were a protest against an art critic who had criticised her for being too 'subjective'[9] and implicitly too female. The scroll she removed was then exhibited, blood stains visible over the typed writing.

The piece performed by Schneemann does what Charcot and Freud were unable to do: to fully understand herself she literally makes her thinking integral to the organ that makes her body female; she does not, and, more importantly, does not want to, separate the two, protesting against the male culture that devalued and wanted to separate the female body and mind.[10] Crucially, she also brings into view what is hidden, the interior of her body becomes exterior without shame, fear, or denial but more as a physical fact that does not need to be hidden away. It is in the lack of 'alluding to' or 'suggestion of' that Schneemann does what Charcot was unable to do with his exposition of the female patient: she integrates her own sexuality and sense of what femininity means to her as a woman without leaving it to the audience to decide what her 'femaleness' should be. In Schneemann's performance she graphically demonstrates and reappropriates what belongs to her, that there is and should be an intimate interplay between the physicality of being female and the mind of being female, rather than carving her body and mind into separate sections as was being required of her to succeed in a male environment—the totality of her mind and body being too much for the men around her. This, of course, is exactly what she wanted to challenge and what is perfectly demonstrated through Charcot's theatre. His female patient is brought out as he performs his version of *Interior Scroll*, with the rather large elephant in the room being that he had limited understanding of what was interior for a woman, but he presumed that he could decide.

For Freud, and what has, on the whole, followed since, the main physical manifestation of having a female body has been ignored. Breasts have been appropriated as 'good' or 'bad' and the vagina in psychoanalysis has traditionally been conceptualised as loss; at best it was 'less than' for Freud. The psychoanalytic gaze towards female anatomy is mainly seen in the context of absence—the absence of a woman having a penis, with a vagina needing a penis to be inserted into it (interestingly I have never come across psychoanalytic writing where the penis is described as needing a vagina into which to insert itself). For psychoanalysis, the vagina has been bathed in absence in all senses where menstruation is the loss of babies rather than the sign of life and vitality, a symbol of a healthy functioning body.

In psychoanalytic literature, there is a well-documented lack of written interest in childbirth,[11] but the real gap in the literature is around menstruation.[12,13] Given the absence of writing about menstruation in psychoanalysis and its lack of inclusion in Freud's theory of psychosexual development, it is perhaps surprising that one of Freud's first intellectual allies, Fleiss, developed a theory about menstruation that saw it as impacting on all areas of life including a male menstruation cycle which lasted twenty-one days.[14] Freud wrote approvingly of the theory but to say he then never quite took up an interest in menstruation and what this meant for women would be a distinct understatement. The great irony is, of course, that most of his patients were women.

When one of the foremost psychoanalysts and challengers to Freudian thinking on psychosexual development, Melanie Klein, came to think about menstruation she doubled down on Freud's ideas of loss; menstruation was the physical manifestation of loss, not just of missing the opportunity to reproduce but also a reminder of not having a penis, 'equivalent in the unconscious to having actually been castrated and having forfeited the possibility of having a child' (p. 306) causing 'disappointments and shocks to her narcissism' (p. 306).[15] For Klein, the inevitable result of this was an increase in hatred from the daughter towards the mother, a return to earlier feelings of anger and guilt for the aggression towards her mother felt during her desire for her father, and for a phallus. The women in this scenario are pitted against each other, the catalyst being the trauma of blood loss which Klein saw as signifying to the young girl that 'the interior of her body and the children contained there have been totally destroyed' (p. 129).[16] In this construction there is no space for a different relationship to take place or even a reversal whereby the mother and daughter are united by a shared experience of development and mutual understanding. Instead the only outcome from this key stage in the girl's development and in the mother–daughter relationship is one where the blood of menstruation is transformed into the bloody battle of competition for supremacy between the women; the only thing to be competed for, of course, is the affection of a man. This is not to say that for some this may be the case, but there also seems to be a passing on of trauma in this formulation. It does not feel too unremarkable for a girl who has been given no understanding of her body or biological development that menstrual blood may well have signified the destruction of the interior of her body and the loss of a child, but for a girl who has been told how her body will develop, this seems unlikely.

In Klein's theory of menstruation there is no outside world beyond the parent's impact on the adolescent daughter. This is possibly symptomatic of the deeply felt taboo and shame about menstruation, that this is something that could not be conceived of as being discussed beyond the immediate family, let alone being understood as a shared experience with other women. It is, perhaps, also symptomatic of the trauma experienced by these women who at that time were left to make sense of their own menstruation and physical development. As young girls, if unprepared, they would not only have to deal with the shock and the inescapably vivid, visual externalising of the internal changes happening to their bodies, but also a sense of abandonment and shame in not having been cared for by another woman who could have understood their experience. In one swift move the young girls risk feeling different and alienated not only from their male friends, brothers, and fathers but also feeling abandoned by their female friends, sisters, and mothers.

A recent study by Donmall[17] of six women's experience of menstruation found that for some the experience of wearing sanitary products made them feel like they were wearing nappies and suggests that this is in accordance with earlier theories about adolescent development such as the regression in adolesence as described by Blos[18] or Chodorow's furthering of a pre-oedipal struggle.[19] Donmall proposes that 'menstruation may reawaken associations with an infantile state of incontinence accompanied by potential feelings of shame, confusion and dependence' (p. 209).[20] This study seems to further the psychoanalytic tropes about women and menstruation, rather than asking the more obvious question of how could women not feel like this when wearing certain sanitary products. There is a startling disavowal in psychoanalysis of the reality of menstruation for women and a continuation of the splitting of the lived experience of women's bodies from their minds.

A brief look at sanitary products in the 1960s, when Blos was writing, and beyond into the 1970s and 80s, shows that sanitary products were like nappies; big and bulky wads of material that sometimes had to be worn attached by a belt. This was in an era well before the much-ridiculed adverts suggesting young girls could skydive or rock climb whilst also menstruating due to the freedom associated with the new versions of sanitary products. Despite some developments, the abhorrence and disgust of periods was written large by the neglect for many years to develop anything more effective than rudimentary dressings to deal with menstrual blood. A popular brand of sanitary towel was called 'Dr White's', giving a pure, unstained, medicalised containment of the shameful red blood, the reality being a thick, unyielding, rectangular wad of material more akin to a medical-style dressing with no consideration for comfort or even female physical anatomy.

Whilst it may be true that for some girls menstruation may be experienced on an unconscious level as a regression to incontinence, this misses that society was treating women as though they had regressed. In the same way as women voicing feelings could be seen as an 'outburst' (something pouring out that should be contained) rather than a woman saying how she is feeling, so women were being treated as an inconvenience for having a menstrual 'outpouring' that needed to be staunched. Even the naming of the products used as 'sanitary' conjures up a medical product to treat an unclean wound; of course that unclean wound was located in the woman and also unseen, unknown, so at any time any woman might be walking around with this unclean wound needing medical attention.

The neglect of the attention of psychoanalysis to the impact of how girls have been treated at this key moment in their lives further demonstrates the relegation of women, that women deserve to be treated in this way, with any feelings of shame, incontinence, or being 'dirty' pathologised as the girl/women's internal world. Any impact menstruation may have on the woman becomes understood as her failings to make sense of her body and the world in

which she lives; there is no trust in women to adequately understand their own experience. This in itself feels like a repetition
and furthering of Freud's contention that women are 'veiled in an
impenetrable obscurity',[21] without asking by whom or for whom
they are 'veiled'.

For Klein, the onset of menstruation meant a further deepening of hatred towards the mother for not giving her child a penis
and bestowing the trauma of menstruation on her. There is no
consideration that the mother might have been the safe place in
which the girl could place her frustration, hoping that the older
woman who had also gone through this process of feeling relegated, dismissed, and seen as dirty, might be able to make sense of
these feelings for the daughter and help her through this process.
The alternative would be to become angry with her father, but,
especially in Klein's times, by that age the adolescent girl would
have already been fully accustomed to the patriarchy in which she
was living, menstruation being a symbol not just of her lacking a
penis but lacking an equal place at the table. It is not surprising
that any girl who might want more than marriage and children
would be disappointed to discover that physical development also
signals getting nearer to a life with increasingly restricted choices.
However, this is also not considered by Klein, instead it is assumed
that it is normal to feel upset at being castrated. In classical psychoanalysis the obvious question never comes next: even if you do
not have a penis, what is so bad about that? It is as though at that
point it becomes agreed to pathologise women's experience and
negatively hallucinate or demonise menstruation.

Perhaps it is understandable that menstruation has been stig-
matised by patriarchal societies as the ramifications of accepting
what women achieve whilst also managing the physical and psychological effects of menstruation would be huge and require a
revolutionary rethink on where strength lies and what constitutes
strength. When listening to a senior male analyst speak of his reasons for entering psychoanalysis, he reflected that as a young man,

one day on a bus journey that he took every day, he realised how radically different he felt this Tuesday to the previous one without any specific events having taken place in the week. At that moment he was struck by the impact of his internal world. This realisation that occurred to him as a young man is, of course, an inescapable realisation for all menstruating young people. As soon as they start having periods they enter a world where their internal world clashes with the external, what was once internal is demonstrably external via the menstrual blood, their menstrual cycle marking continual hormonal and physical changes.

In a piece performed by Casey Jenkins in 2013, titled *Casting Off My Womb,*[22] for a month she inserted rolls of wool into her vagina and knitted every day, making a long white knitted fabric. The colour of the knitted piece changed throughout the month as the wool absorbed her bodily changes. This then became part of her knitted performance, along with the changes she would have to make whilst knitting due to the wool changing in texture, becoming easier or more difficult to use. The performance externalised the artist's daily internal changes and shifts in being, concretising the possibility of creativity held in the uterus, the antithesis of the psychoanalytic void of the vagina. For Casey, her performance was about reclaiming autonomy about her body and how it could be seen and used. Her performance received more than seven million views on YouTube,[23] but the comments left about her performance may give an insight as to why the vagina and menstruation have had to be disavowed by psychoanalysis. Casey went on to make a further exhibition using these comments with a mechanical knitting machine to knit fabrics with the keywords knitted into the pieces. The knitted fabrics represented the repetitive and relentless comments of aggression and hate towards her. It seemed her autonomy and empowerment through not exhibiting shame about her creativity and menstruation was too threatening and unbearable for the thousands of people who left such comments.

Casting Off My Womb and *Interior Scroll* pose a fundamental challenge to Freudian thought and what has continued unchecked into current psychoanalytic thinking. The women are not repudiating the femininity that Freud saw as being required for a successful analysis but transforming what has been seen as a passive, empty female subjectivity into something beyond active, deserving of a place in its own right. What their pieces draw attention to is what has happened to women in society and is paralleled by psychoanalysis' understanding of women and their bodies: a less-than-'void' needing to be filled with a male subjectivity. What Schneemann demonstrates is perhaps the fear from which this assumed male superiority comes, she is able to extract this misogynistic thinking from herself, her vagina remains unmoved by the thinking, the scroll is removed, her blood staining the paper. The scroll is a long narrow strip of paper, smaller still when seen in relation to her naked body, her hands in control of the extraction of this 'thinking' as she removes it from inside herself and in the act of doing so, shows the removal of the thinking from her mind.

When Freud wrote in 'Analysis terminable and interminable'[24] that the repudiation of femininity was the bedrock obstacle to the success of an analysis, it seems that he was alluding to just this struggle between the presumption of superior male subjectivity over female subjectivity—perhaps his own personal bedrock to which he was referring. The women were refusing to accept him inserting his scroll of understanding into them, because there was a fundamental bedrock point missing. How Freud was treating women and conceptualising their distress was innovative and creative until he hit upon his own blind spot and treated women in a way in which these women were well versed and were refusing in the first place—to be treated and reduced to a male understanding of their femininity and female form. What Freud was expecting of them was passivity and acquiescence to his more evolved understanding and psychoanalytic thinking. Instead of Freud becoming frustrated and disappointed with the lack of success of his treatment with these women, what might have been more helpful is if he had considered that they had a view about this too, seeing that they might have something, even something more, than he had to offer rather than seeing women in the light of loss.

It is striking that even in 2018, a leading psychoanalyst, Kohon, continues the psychoanalytic tradition of negatively hallucinating women by failing to see what is obviously apparent. In this case the female genitals: 'In sexual difference, there is always something missing. There are two sexes, each offering the other what the other has not got: a "penis", a "baby"' (p. 271).[25] In this description the male genitals are present, however the female genitals are only present in terms of what they can produce and even that is reduced to one aspect, reproduction. The conception of difference is heavily unbalanced: the penis is not equated to the clitoris, vulva, or vagina, the penis is equated with a baby, which, of course, is reliant on both male and female genitals. The female equivalence is phrased in terms of needing the male counterpart; the vulva and uterus does not exist in its own right.

It is in these ways that female physicality continues to be undermined and seen as less than, in much the same way as women were seen by Freud. These theoretical viewpoints are stated as 'givens' and repeat earlier psychoanalytic mantras, finishing the story prematurely without exploring what more there might be, such as the obvious of what comes before a baby and what this might mean for female development in all ways. For Freud, negatively hallucinating female genitals was a stage to be grown out of,[26] but somehow psychoanalysis has become stuck.

There have been attempts to redress the lack of a place for full female subjectivity within the establishment of psychoanalysis. Nearly ninety years after the International Psychoanalytical Society was founded, in a move to improve the understanding and amount of attention given to women in psychoanalysis, the

British analyst Joan Raphael-Leff founded the first International Psychoanalytical Association's Committee on Women and Psychoanalysis (COWAP) in 1998. Under the International Psychoanalytical Association's own description of the committee, it was set up to 'provide a framework for the exploration of topics relating to issues primarily of concern to women'.[27] What is intriguing is that within just three years of being established the IPA describes the committee as shifting its focus to the 'relations between men and women ... and currently includes issues of concern to men'.[28] It is almost as though despite being an adjunct special interest group on women, even that ground could not be held. The committee's gaze had to turn away from women to look at men; rather than the male gaze of mainstream psychoanalysis turning to look at women, the women's committee had to submit to the need of the patriarchal setting.

It is this negative hallucinating of women that has been well documented in the history of many other disciplines, even more so if the women are of colour, but despite, or perhaps because of, the lack of understanding of women even being documented by Freud and the reification of Freud, the negative hallucinating in psychoanalysis continues unquestioned. On most psychoanalytic training courses, the history of psychoanalysis is given in the same way as history has traditionally been taught, a male whitewash, with the exception of women such as Klein and Anna Freud who have continued the male narrative in psychoanalysis, in Klein's case expounding and deepening the misogyny of Freud.

This is, perhaps, not surprising except that in the same way that menstruation has been scotomised, women and their contributions have been negatively hallucinated or only been seen due to their relation to men. Many times over, psychoanalysis seems to fail the Bechdel test—a test used in analysis of fiction, and based on something first observed by Virginia Woolf, to determine the presence of female characters featuring in their own right rather than being there in relation to men.[29] To name but a few of the female characters in psychoanalysis: Lou Andreas-Salomé was academically extremely accomplished, a published writer, one of the first female psychoanalysts and the first in the psychoanalytic establishment to write about female psychology, she influenced and engaged with thinkers of the time such as Nietzsche and Rilke; Karen Horney was a pioneer in psychoanalytic thinking on women, was one of the founders of the Berlin Psychoanalytic Institute, and later founded her own psychoanalytic training institute; Sabina Spielrein, a psychiatrist and psychoanalyst who over a thirty-year career published more than thirty-five papers in several different languages and was one of the first analysts to research schizophrenia; Margaret Little was a psychiatrist, analyst, and had several admissions to psychiatric hospitals but never missed one day at work, held senior positions at the British Psychoanalytical Society, and made key contributions on the theory of countertransference.

Despite these women making a significant contribution to psychoanalytic thinking, they are perhaps more well known for other reasons. Lou Andreas-Salomé is best known for being a companion to Freud, Karen Horney until recently was best known for her opposition to Freud; Sabina Spielrein is famous for her sexual relationship with Jung; and Margaret Little is primarily referenced for her relationship with Winnicott. It is a shame in more ways than one that these women and the female experience has been negatively hallucinated or selectively seen at best. As Freud described well, a negative hallucination is a radical defence and one that should be given full attention.[30,31] What is needed is for psychoanalysis to take the brave first step of putting itself on the couch to fully grapple with its unconscious fantasies about women and begin coping with what it is working so hard not to see.

Notes

Chapter One

1. Ross, A. (2017). High heels row: Government response 'a cop out' says worker. *The Guardian*, 21 April 2017.
2. Manne, K. (2017). *Down Girl: The Logic of Misogyny*. New York: Oxford University Press.
3. Chodorow, N. J. (2004). Psychoanalysis and women: a personal thirty-five-year retrospect. *Annual of Psychoanalysis, 32*: 101–129.
4. Freud, S. (1926e). The question of lay analysis. *S. E., 20*: 177–258. London: Hogarth.
5. Winnicott, D. W. (1950). Some thoughts on the meaning of the word democracy. *Human Relations, 3*(2): 175–186.
6. Bowlby, J. (1988). *A Secure Base: Parent–Child Attachment and Healthy Human Development*. London: Routledge.

7. Duschinsky, R., Greco, M., & Solomon, J. (2015). The politics of attachment: lines of flight with Bowlby, Deleuze and Guattari. *Theory, Culture and Society*, *32*(7–8): 173–195.

8. Horney, K. (1926). The flight from womanhood: the masculinity-complex in women, as viewed by men and by women. *International Journal of Psychoanalysis*, *7*: 324–339.

9. Freud, S. (1923a). Two encyclopaedia articles. *S. E.*, *18*: 233–260. London: Hogarth.

10. Freud, S. (1908c). On the sexual theories of children. *S. E.*, *9*: 205–226. London: Hogarth.

11. Starr, K. E., & Aron, L. (2011). Women on the couch: Genital stimulation and the birth of psychoanalysis. *Psychoanalytic Dialogues*, *21*(4): 373–392.

12. See note 3.

13. Balsam, R. H. (2015). The war on women in psychoanalytic theory building: past to present. *Psychoanalytic Study of the Child*, *69*: 83–107.

14. See note 3.

15. Cohler, B. J., & Galatzer-Levy, R. (2008). Freud, Anna, and the problem of female sexuality. *Psychoanalytic Inquiry*, *28*(1): 3–26.

16. See note 11.

17. Freud, S. (1923b). *The Ego And The Id. S. E.*, *19*: 1–66. London: Hogarth.

18. Balsam, R. H. (2013). Freud, females, childbirth, and dissidence: Margarete Hilferding, Karen Horney, and Otto Rank. *Psychoanalytic Review*, *100*(5): 695–716.

19. See note 4.

20. Horney, K. (1924). On the genesis of the castration complex in women. *International Journal of Psychoanalysis*, *5*: 50–65.

21. See note 13.

22. Fliegel, Z. O. (1973). Feminine psychosexual development in Freudian theory: a historical reconstruction. *Psychoanalytic Quarterly*, *42*(3): 385–408.

23. See note 18.

24. See note 22.

25. I have used the term patient to refer to the person who comes to see the psychotherapist. Whilst the term patient carries certain connotations with which I do not agree, the other commonly used terms—client, analysand, customer, service user—are equally inadequate.

26. Hirsch, D. (2018). Unconscious pacts and the bisexuality of the countertransference in the treatment. In: R. J. Perelberg (Ed.), *Psychic Bisexuality: A British–French Dialogue* (pp. 170–188). London & New York: Routledge.

27. Balsam, R. H. (2015). Provides a clear and insightful overview of the contributions of different writers who have challenged classical thinking on women throughout the history of psychoanalysis.

28. Orbach, S. (1978). *Fat is a Feminist Issue: The Anti-diet Guide to Permanent Weight Loss*. New York: Paddington Press.

29. See note 13.

30. From personal communication with Rosemary Balsam.

31. https: //www.sigourneyaward.org/recipients-1 (last accessed 28 September 2021).

Chapter Two

1. Abramović, M. (1974). *Rhythm 0* (performance art). Studio Morra, Naples.

2. O'Hagan, S. (2010). Interview: Marina Abramović. *The Guardian*, 3 October. https://www.theguardian.com/artanddesign/2010/oct/03/interview-marina-abramovic-performance-artist

3. Freud, S. (1920g). *Beyond The Pleasure Principle. S. E., 18*: 1–64. London: Hogarth.

4. Freud, S. (1914c). On narcissism: an introduction. *S. E., 14*: 67–102. London: Hogarth.

5. Tronick, E. Z., Als, H., & Adamson, L. (1979). Structure of early face-to-face communicative interactions. In: M. Bullowa (Ed.), *Before Speech: The Beginning of Interpersonal Communication* (pp. 349–372). Cambridge: Cambridge University Press.

6. A clip of a baby's response to the still face experiment with a commentary by Ed Tronick can be seen on https: //youtu.be/apzXGEbZht0

7. Winnicott, D. W. (1952). Anxiety associated with insecurity. In: *Through Paediatrics to Psycho-Analysis: Collected Papers* (pp. 97–100). London: Hogarth Press and The Institute of Psychoanalysis, 1975.

8. Winnicott, D. W. (1960). The theory of the parent–infant relationship. *International Journal of Psychoanalysis, 41*: 585–595.

9. Bion, W. R. (1962). The psycho-analytic study of thinking. *International Journal of Psychoanalysis, 43*: 306–310.

10. See note 2.

11. Freud, S. (1910k). "Wild" psycho-analysis. *S. E., 11*: 219–228. London: Hogarth.

12. Winnicott, D. W. (1950). Some thoughts on the meaning of the word democracy. *Human Relations, 3*(2): 175–186.

13. A UK-wide report by the British Medical Association (BMA) in 2021 found that 91% of female doctors had experienced sexism at work. A 2021 report focusing on the situation in Wales found that 86% of Welsh doctors agreed there is an issue of sexism in the NHS, whilst 70% felt that this acted as a barrier to career progression (Sexism in medicine: a close look at the situation in Wales, https://www.bma.org.uk/news-and-opinion/sexism-in-medicine-a-closer-look-at-the-situation-in-wales (last accessed 29 September 2021)). Doctors involved in the survey reported being ignored by other doctors in favour of their male colleagues, endless mansplaining, and being talked over (BBC News, Sexism in the workplace: women scared to speak out in NHS, https://www.bbc.com/news/uk-wales-58408550 (last accessed 29 September 2021)).

14. Haridasani Gupta, A. (2020). It's not just you: in online meetings, many women can't get a word in. *The New York Times*, 14 April, https://www.nytimes.com/2020/04/14/us/zoom-meetings-gender.html. This article describes the impact of moving to online meetings due to the pandemic. It describes the experience of many women in America during online meetings and the increasing difficulty in their views being heard.

15. IPA Organisational Officers Past and Current. https://www.ipa.world/ IPA/en/IPA1/officers_past_and_current/ipa_officers_past_and_current.aspx (last accessed 21 September 2021).

16. Information provided by email from The British Society of Psychoanalysis.

17. Palmer, S. (2015). Controversial Discussions for the XXIst Century. *PEP Videogrants, 1*: 2. This is a film of interviews with various prominent members of the International Psychoanalytical Association. It is especially of interest for the way in which Melanie Klein's physicality is discussed.

18. Brown, S. (2017). Is counselling women's work? *Therapy Today, 28*(2).

19. UKCP (Wikipedia page). https://en.wikipedia.org/wiki/United_ Kingdom_Council_for_Psychotherapy (last accessed 28 September 2021).

Chapter Three

1. Palmer, S. (2015). Controversial Discussions for the XXIst Century. *PEP Videogrants, 1*: 2.

2. Freud, S. (1923b). *The Ego And The Id. S. E., 19*: 1–66. London: Hogarth.

3. Freud, S. (1925j). Some psychical consequences of the anatomical distinction between the sexes. *S. E., 19*: 241–258. London: Hogarth.

4. Fliegel, Z. O. (1973). Feminine psychosexual development in Freudian theory: a historical reconstruction. *Psychoanalytic Quarterly, 42*(3): 385–408.

5. Balsam, R. H. (2013). Freud, females, childbirth, and dissidence: Margarete Hilferding, Karen Horney, and Otto Rank. *Psychoanalytic Review, 100*(5): 695–716.

6. Clara Thompson wrote several papers contesting Freud's views of women and arguing for women to be understood within the cultural and social context in which they were living. She directly contests Freud's view of penis envy in her paper in 1943: "Penis envy" in women. *Psychiatry, 6*(2): 123–125.

7. Mitchell, J. (1974). *Psychoanalysis and Feminism: Freud, Reich, Laing and Women.* New York: Pantheon Books.

8. Kulish, N., & Holtzman, D. (2008). *A Story of Her Own: The Female Oedipus Complex Reexamined and Renamed.* New York: Jason Aronson.

9. Benjamin, J. (2015). Masculinity, complex: a historical take. *Studies in Gender and Sexuality, 16*(4): 271–277.

10. Balsam, R. H. (2015). The war on women in psychoanalytic theory building: past to present. *Psychoanalytic Study of the Child, 69*: 83–107.

11. Freud, S. (1925j). Some psychical consequences of the anatomical distinction between the sexes. *S. E., 19*: 241–258. London: Hogarth.

12. Ibid.

13. Heilman, M. E., Wallen, A. S., Fuchs, D., & Tamkins, M. M. (2004). Penalties for success: reactions to women who succeed at male gender-typed tasks. *Journal of Applied Psychology, 89*(3): 416–427.

14. See note 5.

15. Steiner, J. (2011). *Seeing and Being Seen: Emerging from a Psychic Retreat.* Abingdon, Oxon: Routledge.

Chapter Four

1. Bion, W. R. (1967). Notes on memory and desire. *Psychoanalytic Forum, 2*: 279–290.

2. Winnicott, D. W. (1950). Some thoughts on the meaning of the word 'democracy'. In: C. Winnicott, R. Shepherd & M. Davis (Eds.), *Home is Where We Start From: Essays by a Psychoanalyst* (pp. 239–259). Harmondsworth: Penguin, 1986. Also in *Human Relations, 3*(2): 175–186.

3. Horney, K. (1926). The flight from womanhood: the masculinity-complex in women, as viewed by men and by women. *International Journal of Psychoanalysis, 7*: 324–339.

4. Freud, S. (1908c). On the sexual theories of children. *S. E., 9*: 205–226. London: Hogarth.

5. Freud, S. (1910a). Five lectures on psycho-analysis. *S. E.*, *11*: 1–56. London: Hogarth.

6. Kanner, L. (1943). Autistic disturbances of affective contact. *The Nervous Child*, *2*: 217–250 (reprinted in 1968 in *Acta Paedopsychiatrica*, *35*(4): 100–136).

7. Bettelheim, B. (1967). *The Empty Fortress: Infantile Autism and The Birth of the Self*. New York: Free Press.

8. Tustin, F. (1994). Autistic children who are assessed as not brain-damaged. *Journal of Child Psychotherapy*, *20*(1): 103–131.

9. Winnicott, D. W. (1956). Primary maternal preoccupation. In: *Through Paediatrics to Psycho-Analysis: Collected Papers*. London: Hogarth Press and The Institute of Psychoanalysis, 1975.

Chapter Five

1. Brouillet, P. A. (1887). *A Clinical Lesson at the Salpêtrière*. Musée d'Histoire de la Médecine, Paris, France.

2. Starr, K. E., & Aron, L. (2011). Women on the couch: Genital stimulation and the birth of psychoanalysis. *Psychoanalytic Dialogues*, *21*(4): 373–392.

3. Ibid.

4. Freud, S. (1923b). *The Ego And The Id. S. E.*, *19*: 1–66. London: Hogarth.

5. Criado Perez, C. (2019). *Invisible Women: Exposing Data Bias in a World Designed for Men*. London: Vintage.

6. Freud, S. (1923e). The infantile genital organization (an interpolation into the theory of sexuality). *S. E.*, *19*: 139–146. London: Hogarth.

7. Freud, S. (1940a [1938]). An outline of psycho-analysis. *S. E.*, *23*: 139–208. London: Hogarth.

8. Schneemann, C. (1975). *Interior Scroll*. Performed at *Women Here and Now* art exhibition in East Hampton, New York.

9. Moreland, Q. (2015). Forty years of Carolee Schneemann's "Interior Scroll". *Hyperallergic*. https://hyperallergic.com/232342/forty-years-of-carolee-schneemanns-interior-scroll/

10. Horne, V. (2020). 'The personal clutter … the painterly mess …' Tracing a history of Carolee Schneemann's *Interior Scroll. Art History*, 43(5): 984–1006.

11. Balsam, R. H. (2015). The war on women in psychoanalytic theory building: past to present. *Psychoanalytic Study of the Child*, 69: 83–107.

12. Donmall, K. (2013). What it means to bleed: an exploration of young women's experiences of menarche and menstruation. *British Journal of Psychotherapy*, 29(2): 202–216.

13. Kolod, S. (2010). The menstrual cycle as a subject of psychoanalytic inquiry. *Journal of the American Academy of Psychoanalysis and Dynamic Psychiatry*, 38(1): 77–98.

14. Lupton, M. J. (1993). *Menstruation and Psychoanalysis*. Urbana, IL: University of Illinois Press. Lupton gives a comprehensive history of menstruation in psychoanalysis with the varied ways in which it has been addressed and overlooked. To my knowledge this is a vastly under-used resource.

15. Klein, M. (1932). *The Psycho-Analysis of Children*. London: Hogarth.

16. Ibid.

17. See note 12.

18. Blos, P. (1962). *On Adolescence: A Psychoanalytic Interpretation.* London: Free Press.

19. Chodorow, N. (1978). *The Reproduction of Mothering: Psychoanalysis and the Sociology of Gender.* Berkeley, CA: University of California Press.

20. See note 12.

21. Freud, S. (1905d). *Three Essays on the Theory of Sexuality. S. E.*, 7: 123–246. London: Hogarth.

22. Jenkins, C. (2013). *Casting Off My Womb* (performance art). Darwin Visual Arts Association.

23. Jenkins, C. (2013). I'm the 'vaginal knitting' performance artist—and I want to defend my work. *The Guardian*, 17 December 2013. https://www.theguardian.com/commentisfree/2013/dec/17/vaginal-knitting-artist-defence

24. Freud, S. (1937c). Analysis terminable and interminable. *S. E.*, *23*: 209–254. London: Hogarth.

25. Kohon, G. (2018). Bye-bye, sexuality. In: R. J. Perelberg *Psychic Bisexuality: A British–French dialogue* (pp. 258–276). London & New York: Routledge.

26. Freud, S. (1925j). Some psychical consequences of the anatomical distinction between the sexes. *S. E.*, *19*: 241–258. London: Hogarth.

27. IPA COWAP. www.ipa.world/ipa/en/Committees/Committee_detail.aspx?code=COWAP (last accessed 21 September 2021).

28. Ibid.

29. Bechdel test. www.bechdeltestfest.com

30. Freud, S. (1917d). A metapsychological supplement to the theory of dreams. *S. E.*, *14*: 217–235. London: Hogarth.

31. Freud, S. (1925h). Negation. *S. E.*, *19*: 233–240. London: Hogarth.

Acknowledgements

Getting this book to publication has not been a straightforward process, but the experience has been instructive in proving that now more than ever there is a need for misogyny in psychoanalysis to be addressed. I would particularly like to thank Kate Pearce at Phoenix Publishing House for having the freedom of thought to publish this book and with such good humour and warmth.

I am very grateful to Debbie Zimmerman and Dr Louise Hood for their endless support and belief in the need for me to write this book and in my capacity to do it. I would also like to thank them for sharing their wealth of experience and making playing with ideas so enjoyable, expansive and most importantly fun.

Jacqueline Glynn, Lawrence Kilshaw, and Theresa Plewman have been invaluable in providing a space to develop my thinking and finding much needed humour at difficult junctures.

Spending time with Brooke Morris, Michelle Devine, Paul Mowat, and Gina Gründlich is a constant reminder of the importance of living life on your own terms and the freedom of a life that prioritises connection with others.

I am extremely grateful to Adam Phillips for his encouragement, generosity of interest in my writing, and for enabling me to go beyond my own internalised misogyny to take a seat at the table. My conversations with him are always immensely enjoyable and instrumental in expanding my thinking and writing.

Daniel Jenkinson is always my first reader, his thinking, kindness, and humour sustain me throughout. I am hugely thankful to my children for their uncompromising honesty, laughter, and for giving me hope in a generation that sees strength in a world less binary.

About the author

Michaela Chamberlain trained at the Bowlby Centre and also studied in the Psychoanalytic Unit at UCL. Shortly after qualifying at the Bowlby Centre in 2016, she started teaching Freud and attachment theory and became CEO of the Bowlby Centre. She worked as an honorary psychotherapist in two NHS Trusts for several years. She has presented clinical papers at public forums and has been published in the journal *Attachment: New Directions in Psychotherapy and Relational Psychoanalysis*. She is currently carrying out a doctoral research project on a psychoanalytic reading of gendered blood in live art and psychoanalytic writing at Roehampton University.

She is currently in private practice as a psychoanalytic psychotherapist and is a supervisor and training therapist.

Index